acrylic pour painting

acrylic pour painting

A BEGINNER'S GUIDE WITH INSTRUCTIONS, IDEAS, AND TIPS FOR CREATING UNIQUE ABSTRACT PAINTINGS

CARRIE KELLEY

Legal Disclaimer

The information in this book is accurate to the best of the author's knowledge. Personalized guidance for those with specific concerns, or for individuals with health conditions, should be sought from an appropriate professional.

The reader of this book accepts all liability for any and all unintended consequences that may occur due to the use of the information provided, including but not limited to damage, injury, or loss of persons or property.

Individual results of artwork may vary. The author makes no guarantee of the outcome or quality of artwork created using this information.

The instructions in this book were written for adults.

If any inaccuracies have occurred, they will be addressed in future editions.

The names of manufacturers, brands, product lines, and products mentioned in this book are for informational purposes only. No intent to infringe on any copyrights or trademarks is intended. Brand names and trademarks are the property of their respective owners.

contents

CHAPTER 1

introduction

ACRYLIC POUR PAINTING IS A FUN AND EASY WAY TO CREATE ONE-OF-A-kind abstract artwork. Individuals at every skill level can enjoy this fascinating type of painting, from those who've never painted before to experienced artists and everyone in between. Whether you're interested in exploring pour painting as a hobby or have professional goals in mind, with the right supplies and a little know-how, you'll be on your way to pouring your first colorful creation.

I'm an experienced acrylic painter and fluid artist who wrote this guide to help new pour painters get started with this innovative style of painting. Although pouring isn't difficult, learning the basics unique to this art form is the first step toward being able to create pieces you love. From paints and preparation to the pouring process and beyond, some advance knowledge and insight will give you the confidence to experiment with the multitude of inventive techniques acrylic pour painting offers.

The guide begins with a beginner-focused overview of pour painting basics. You'll learn about choosing paints and colors, pouring medium and painting surface options, the ideal workspace, and commonsense tips to paint safely.

Next, I provide a simple, quick-start tutorial and painting recipe for absolute beginners or anyone who'd like to try pour painting with a minimal number of budget-friendly supplies and a few easy steps.

My detailed supply list covers all the pouring must-haves and optional items for edge touch-ups, varnishing, framing, and other products for specific techniques or adding creative effects to your art.

And because a successful painting begins with a properly prepared surface, I teach the steps to make canvases, wood panels, and other painting surfaces pour-ready.

Once you're ready to paint, you'll learn the essentials of paint mixing, optimal paint consistency, and paint-to-pouring medium ratios. Then, you'll find step-by-step instructions for several popular pour painting techniques, including the dirty flip cup pour, the puddle pour, and a beach pour.

Since there's more to do once a painting is finished, this book covers post-painting clean-up and the various options to protect a completed work and get it ready to show off.

With the pro tips and suggestions throughout, you'll discover ways to avoid common pouring pitfalls so you can learn how to produce paintings you're happy with.

Because I'm sure you'll love this type of art as much as I do, I've included an assortment of ideas for future projects, including color combination ideas and how to make beverage coasters using poured paint.

As a bonus, I've added a chapter about how to start a pour painting journal. Recording some notes about each painting is a simple yet effective way to identify what materials and methods create your best work and what improvements to make to become a better painter more quickly.

Most importantly, you'll gain the fundamental skills to create your own unique art and be prepared to explore the many new pouring techniques that continue to emerge.

If you're ready to dive into the colorful and magical world of acrylic pour painting, let's get started!

what is acrylic pour painting?

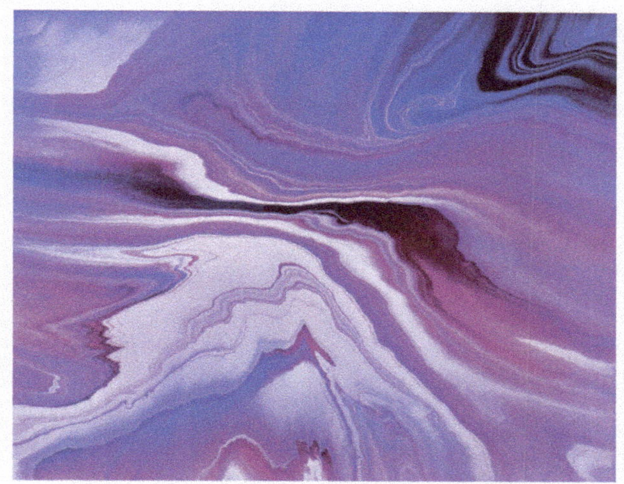

ACRYLIC POUR PAINTING IS A PAINTING METHOD IN WHICH VARIOUS techniques and tools are used to pour and manipulate fluid acrylic paint to create abstract paintings and other artwork. This captivating painting style lets the paint flow and colors interact, resulting in colorful art with unexpected designs and patterns that are impossible to make with a paintbrush. Unlike a traditional acrylic painting, which can take a while to finish, pour painting lets individuals complete a piece of artwork in minutes.

Pour Painting's Origins

Many assume pour painting is a novel style of art because of its popularity in recent years, but this technique has been seen as far back as the 1930s in the work of Mexican artist David Alfaro Siqueiros. Since then, many artists worldwide have used similar fluid painting techniques in their art. One of the most notable is American abstract expressionist Jackson Pollock, who used a drip painting technique in many of his most iconic works.

The Infinite Possibilities of Pour Painting

Acrylic pour painting can be used for an array of artistic endeavors. From paintings and mixed media art projects to decorating rocks and jewelry-making, this art style gives artists (and aspiring ones) a colorful way to express their creative spirit.

Whether on their own or in groups, at painting parties or classes, millions of people worldwide have embraced this exciting art form to make vibrant paintings for fun, to give as gifts, or to sell.

Although there are countless ways to create with pour painting, they all have one thing in common: it's always a surprise to see the ultimate result.

an overview of acrylic paints for pouring

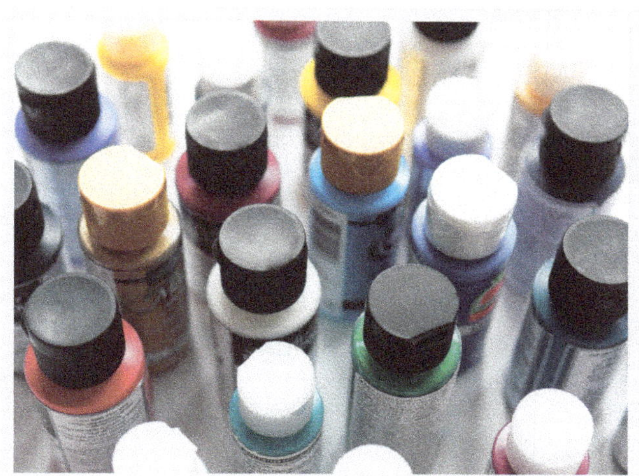

THE SPECIFIC PAINT USED FOR A PAINTING SIGNIFICANTLY AFFECTS THE overall appearance and quality of the finished artwork. To help you choose paints for your pours, this chapter focuses on the need-to-know essentials about acrylic paint.

WHAT IS ACRYLIC PAINT?

Acrylic paint is a quick-drying, water-soluble type of paint. Once dry, acrylics are flexible, water-resistant, and durable. Because of its versatility, people of all skill levels use acrylic paint for many types of creative endeavors.

CHOOSING ACRYLIC PAINTS FOR POURING

Here are the key factors to consider when selecting paints.

Viscosity

One of the first considerations when deciding which paints to use is viscosity. Viscosity refers to the paint's consistency. Low viscosity paints are thin, and high viscosity paints are thick. Although all types of acrylic paint can be made usable for pouring, low viscosity acrylics are the easiest to work with because they're already in a pourable form. These paints are typically in bottles and include:

- **Liquid, Fluid, or Free Flow Acrylics** - Thin and flowing acrylics
- **Soft Body Acrylics** - Creamy paint that's just slightly thicker than fluid or liquid acrylics
- **High Flow Acrylics** - Very thin but concentrated paints with an ink-like consistency

The paints listed above are not watered-down versions of thicker acrylics. Despite a thinner formulation, they contain the same amount of color pigment as high viscosity paints.

Heavy body acrylics, which are high viscosity paints in tubes, also work for pouring, but it takes a few additional steps to make them thin enough to pour.

The viscosity of medium body acrylics is between soft body and heavy body paints.

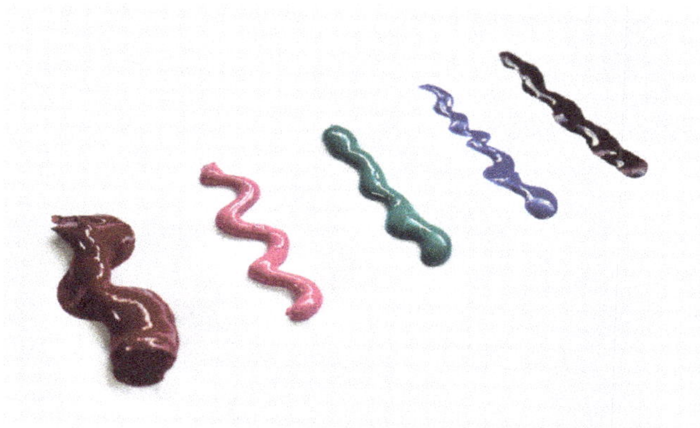

*Several types of acrylic paint, from left: Heavy Body, Soft Body,
Fluid, High Flow, Acrylic Ink*

I suggest opting for paints in a fluid, liquid, or soft body formulation to keep things simple when you're a new painter. If you already have heavy body acrylics, Chapter 15 (Section 10) explains how to prepare these for pouring.

Other Key Qualities of Acrylic Paint

The labels on the bottles or tubes of paint usually provide details that can be helpful as you make your selections. Here are a few qualities you'll likely see and why they matter.

Opacity - A paint's opacity refers to how much light can pass through it.

- **Opaque** - Full coverage
- **Semi-Opaque** - Partial coverage
- **Translucent or Semi-Transparent** - Partially see-through
- **Transparent** - Fully see-through

The opacity of each paint color affects the others and the overall look of a painting. Opaque colors completely block out the hues beneath them, while non-opaque shades allow other colors to be revealed in varying degrees.

Translucent colors can look beautiful in pours, but shades appear less intense than in the bottle when poured over darker colors.

Tip: A translucent or transparent paint color can be made opaquer by mixing it with white or another opaque shade.

There are no rules about using paints of different opacities in a painting. A mix of opaque and non-opaque paints creates beautiful effects when the colors flow and blend, although using all opaque or all translucent colors also makes interesting artwork.

Finish - A paint's finish can be described as one of the below.

- **Glossy** - A shiny finish
- **Satin** - A subtle shine
- **Matte** - A flat, shine-free finish

A paint's final finish can also be affected by the pouring medium it's combined with, but this varies by product combination.

If a painting's finish is uneven or you wish to change it, just add a coat of varnish or finishing spray after the artwork is fully dry.

Lightfastness or Permanence - This refers to a paint's ability to withstand UV light without fading over time. Many paint bottle labels have numbers or symbols to indicate how lightfast the product is. This will vary by brand.

Painters pouring for fun or practice don't need to be as concerned about lightfastness as someone who wants their paintings to last for a long time.

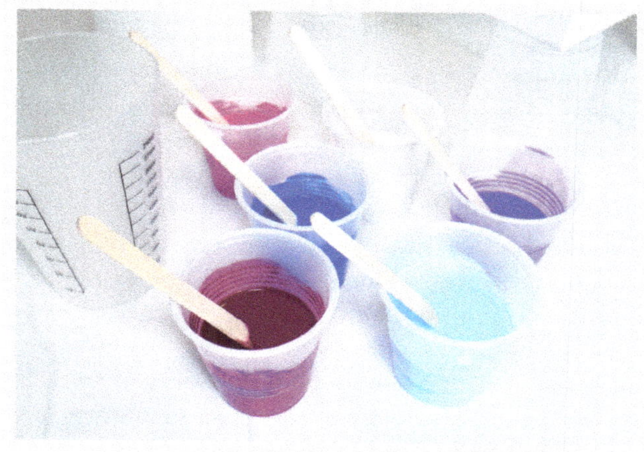

DIFFERENCES IN ACRYLIC PAINT QUALITY

Not all acrylic paints are the same. They differ in quality, cost, and how long artwork created with them will last without color changes or fading. Here's an overview of several qualities of acrylic paint used for pouring.

Artist Grade Acrylic Paints

Artist grade acrylics, also called professional grade acrylics, are highly pigmented paints in a wide spectrum of colors. Because they're so concentrated, a small amount of paint goes a long way. They're also more lightfast than lesser quality paints. These high-quality acrylics are ideal for creating archival quality pour paintings with vibrant hues.

Student Grade Acrylic Paints

Student grade acrylics have a lower price point than artist paints, which makes them a popular option for new painters. Although they come in a wide range of qualities, some student paints rival the color intensity and overall experience of working with artist grade acrylics.

As with all paints, I suggest reading product reviews or asking for recommendations to find the best ones for your art.

Craft Acrylic Paints

Craft acrylic paints are designed for various arts and crafts projects, but since their consistency is similar to low and medium viscosity paints, they can be used for pouring too.

There are a few things to be aware of when using this type of paint for your art. Although craft acrylics are inexpensive, they lack the vivid colors and long-term durability of artist grade paints. It also takes more paint to achieve the same level of color intensity.

You may also find that the quality and viscosity of craft acrylic paints can vary from brand to brand and even bottle to bottle, with some colors being much thicker or thinner than others.

That said, craft acrylics can still produce beautiful paintings. They're a budget-friendly option for beginners and great to use when learning new pouring techniques.

OTHER ACRYLIC PAINT OPTIONS FOR POURING

Pre-Mixed Acrylic Paints for Pouring - Pre-mixed acrylic paints made for pouring are ready to use without adding a pouring medium. While they offer the convenience of skipping the step of mixing paint, they're not the best option for painters who enjoy experimenting with different pouring mediums to add specific effects to their art.

Acrylic Inks - Acrylic inks are very concentrated and ultra-fluid. Small amounts can be mixed with a pouring medium and used for a painting. Just like acrylic paints, inks are available in transparent, translucent, and opaque shades. Many are water-resistant or waterproof.

Metallic Acrylic Paints - Some paint brands offer a selection of metallic, iridescent, and pearlescent paints that add an eye-catching sparkle to a painting. These paints can be used on their own or mixed with non-metallic colors for a more subtle shine. They add fascinating effects to works, even when just used as an accent but don't expect to see their full sparkle until they're dry.

TIPS FOR CHOOSING ACRYLIC PAINTS

- Choosing paint is a matter of preference and budget. Since artist grade paints can be expensive, many beginners prefer to start with student or craft acrylics. Others prefer to use artist grade paints from the start. Both options are fine, so choose what's best for you.
- If you're unsure what brand of paints to buy, the painting department staff in art supply stores and online product reviews may provide guidance.
- Always read labels to be clear on what you're buying.
- No matter what paints you decide to use, consider buying a limited supply until you're sure you're happy with them.

SHELF LIFE OF ACRYLIC PAINTS

Most acrylic paints can last several years, assuming they're properly stored. This means keeping them at an average room temperature, away from direct sunlight and heat sources, and with the caps tightly sealed. If it's been a while since they were used, check to ensure they're not dry, thick, or grainy. If this is the case, they're unusable.

WHERE TO BUY ACRYLIC PAINTS

Artist, student, and craft acrylic paints are sold at arts & crafts supply stores and online. Craft acrylics are often available in discount stores' arts & crafts aisle.

choosing colors for fluid artwork

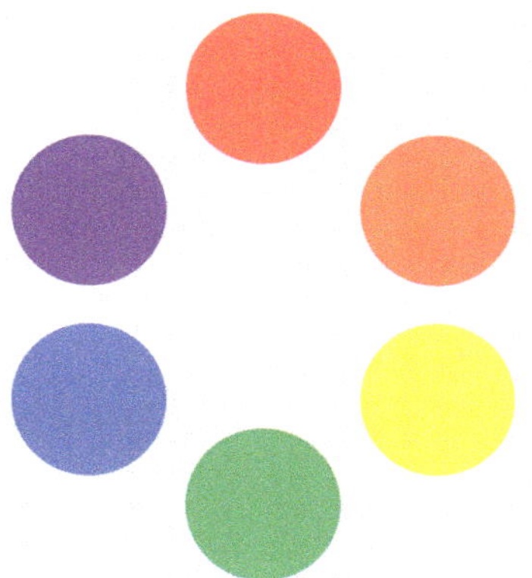

COLOR IS ONE OF THE FIRST THINGS PEOPLE NOTICE ABOUT A PIECE OF ART. The artist's selections determine whether the work will be bold and vibrant, soft and understated, or dark and dramatic. While it's unnecessary to be a color expert to choose hues for acrylic pours, learning a few basics and understanding the unique considerations for selecting shades for fluid art can enable you to make the most of color in your paintings.

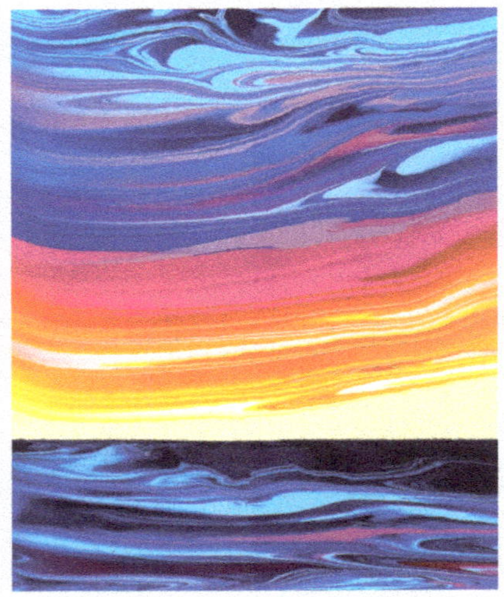

COLOR 101

If you're new to color fundamentals, a **color wheel** is the simplest way to understand color, color relationships, and what colors to mix to create new colors. This indispensable artists' tool is sold at art supply stores and online.

Primary Colors

There are three primary colors. These pure colors can't be made from any other shades.

- Red
- Yellow
- Blue

Secondary Colors

Secondary colors are created by mixing two primary colors.

- Orange (Red + Yellow)
- Green (Yellow + Blue)
- Violet (Red + Blue)

Tertiary Colors

Tertiary colors can be made by mixing one primary and its adjacent secondary color.

- Red-Orange
- Yellow-Orange
- Yellow-Green
- Blue-Green
- Blue-Violet
- Red-Violet

Tints, Tones, Shades

Besides mixing different colors to create new ones, colors can be altered by adding white, black, or gray.

- **Tint** - A color plus white
- **Tone** - A color plus gray
- **Shade** - A color plus black

Color Temperature

Color temperature is the warmth or coolness of a color. Red, orange, and yellow are considered warm colors. Cool shades are green, blue, and purple. White, black, gray, and beige fall into the neutral category. There are also warm shades of cool colors and cool shades of warm colors, such as a cool red (magenta) or a warm green (chartreuse).

For your first paintings, selecting either all warm or all cool shades can prevent the muddiness that sometimes occurs when complementary colors (colors opposite each other on the color wheel) come together. Warm and cool colors can be combined in a painting, but using an assortment of hues can take practice.

No matter what colors are being considered, determine whether they are warm or cool versions of a particular shade. For example, a bluish (cool) purple is less likely to appear muddy alongside a bluish (cool) green than pairing a warm purple with a cool green.

There are exceptions to every rule, and artists frequently make even the most unlikely combinations work, so practice is vital.

Color Value and Creating Contrast

Color value refers to the relative lightness or darkness of a color. In pour painting, using some light, medium, and darker shades creates stronger contrast between colors and accentuates the unique patterns and designs that develop in the wet paint.

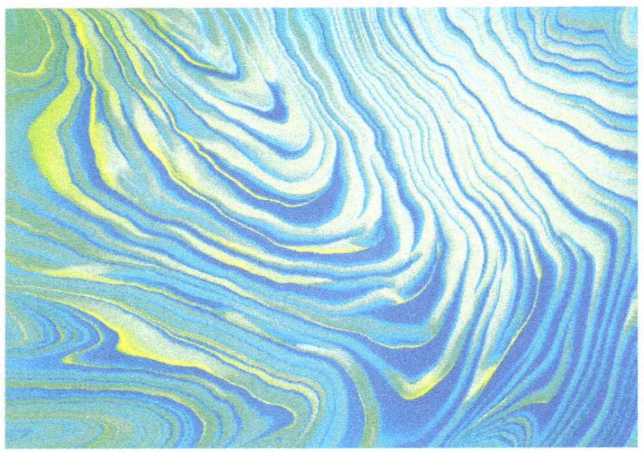

COLOR CHANGES AFTER POURING

There are often color changes that occur before a painting dries. You'll likely notice differences if you take a photo of a freshly poured painting and another after it's dry. There are several reasons for this. Unlike traditional acrylic painting, where paint is applied with a brush and stays in place, fluid colors on a painting surface take on a life of their own. As the hues flow and blend, new colors often form. Some shades may become more or less prominent, and the overall appearance of the artwork changes to some extent.

Color changes also occur when dense paint colors sink and less dense colors rise toward the surface. Additionally, some paints turn darker as they dry.

While it's impossible to predict how colors will interact and change after they've been poured, with a bit of practice, you'll get a better sense of what to expect from certain hues and combinations.

WORKING WITH INTENSE COLORS

Dark or intense paint colors often overpower lighter shades in a painting. These include black, brown, deep blues, purples, and red. Unless you want a piece of art with primarily dark or intense tones, limit the amount of these shades until you see how they appear in a finished painting.

HOW MANY COLORS TO USE IN A PAINTING

Pour paintings look beautiful with just a few hues or many. It takes at least two colors or two shades of a single color for a painting, but there's no limit to the number of colors to use.

I suggest starting with three or four colors. As you become more familiar with choosing and mixing colors, consider using four to seven (or even more) in a painting.

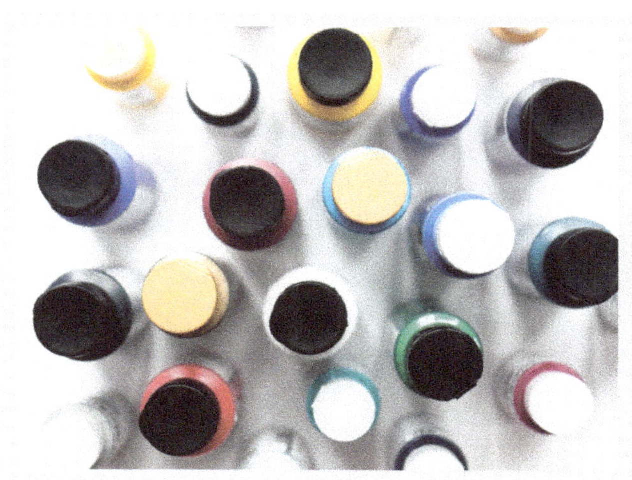

HOW MANY PAINT COLORS TO BUY

I recommend buying at least three to six colors you think will look good together, plus a bottle or two of white and black to add contrast or to lighten or darken colors.

Another option is to purchase a starter acrylic paint set with six to twelve shades. Most starter sets have primary colors which can be mixed to create new shades, as explained at the beginning of this chapter.

It's also helpful to have a few extra bottles of your favorite color or colors because you'll likely use these frequently.

COLOR SCHEMES

Color schemes are combinations of colors chosen because of how they coordinate and accent each other. Here are two beginner-friendly color scheme ideas to try.

Monochromatic Color Scheme

A monochromatic color scheme uses multiple tints, tones, or shades of a single color.

Example #1: Violet, Medium Violet, Pale Violet

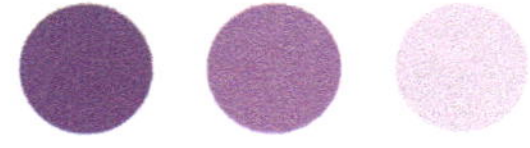

Example #2: Dark Blue, Medium Blue, Light Blue

Analogous Color Scheme

An analogous color scheme uses two to five colors that sit beside each other on the color wheel. This color scheme is a simple way to select hues that will coordinate well.

Example #1: Blue, Blue-Violet, Violet, Red-Violet

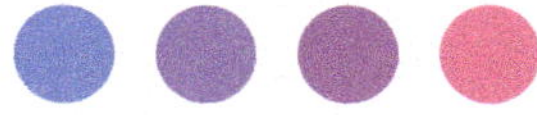

Example #2: Blue, Blue-Green, Green, Yellow-Green

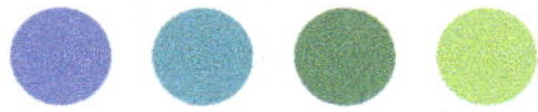

Tip: With any color scheme, use white as an additional color for even more contrast between shades.

COLOR COMBINATION IDEAS

Here are a few ideas if you need more inspiration for color combinations. If you're new to fluid art, you may find it easier to begin with a limited color palette and then expand to a broader mix of shades after you've finished a few pieces.

Tip: It's unnecessary to use these colors in equal parts; just experiment and make the combos your own.

Black, White, and Gold Combo

- Black
- White
- Iridescent or Metallic Gold

Blue and Gold Combo

- Dark Blue or Navy
- Aqua
- Iridescent or Metallic Gold
- White

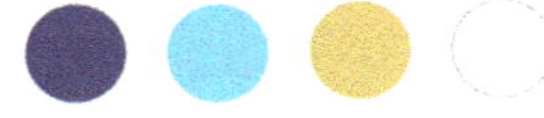

Purple and Gold Combo

- Purple or Plum
- Medium or Light Pink
- Iridescent or Metallic Gold
- White

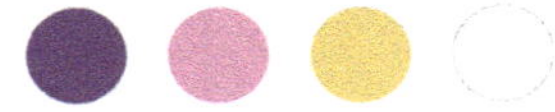

Purple, Blue, and Aqua Combo

- Purple
- Medium Blue
- Aqua
- White or Iridescent White

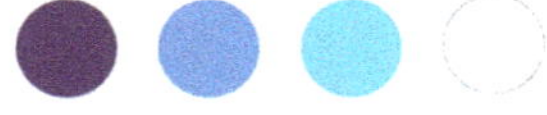

Blues and Silver Combo

- Dark Blue or Navy
- Aqua
- Light Blue
- Iridescent or Metallic Silver
- White

Blue and Green Combo

- Phthalo Blue (Green Shade)
- Phthalo Green (Blue Shade)
- White
- Iridescent or Metallic Silver

Pink, Blues, and Silver Combo

- Pale Pink
- Prussian Blue or Dark Blue
- Light Blue
- Iridescent or Metallic Silver
- White

MY COLOR TIPS

- There's no need to overthink color. Choosing colors can be as simple as lining up a few paint bottles to see how the shades coordinate.
- Give any regular paint color a metallic shimmer by mixing in some metallic paint.
- If you like bright, bold hues, use one or more fluorescent or neon shades in your painting.
- Get a bottle of iridescent white. This beautiful, pearl-like shade can be used on its own or to lighten other colors while adding a metallic sparkle.
- Don't be afraid to experiment with any new color combinations ideas you have. Whether it's a hit or a miss, you'll learn something for future paintings.
- Everyone has certain hues they're drawn to. Try experimenting with your favorite colors in your art.
- If you're unsure about a color combination and aren't ready to try it on a large canvas, make a mini "test" painting on a small canvas panel, a piece of cardboard, or a half sheet from a canvas pad. This will allow you to preview the results before investing time and supplies on a large painting.
- There are countless sources of inspiration for color ideas. A few possibilities include nature, landscapes, cityscapes, the sky, floral arrangements, fashion, fabrics, plants, flower gardens, and galaxies.

CHAPTER 5

all about pouring medium

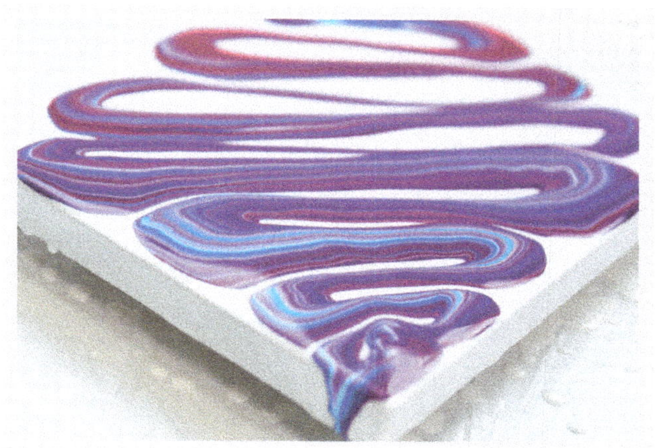

A POURING MEDIUM IS A FLUID PRODUCT MIXED WITH ACRYLIC PAINTS before pouring. It helps the paint move freely across the painting surface while aiding in keeping colors separate, so they don't blend into a muddy tone when the colors interact. Pouring mediums also help level the paint to create a smooth surface, extend paint volume without diluting color, and help prevent paint from cracking or crazing as it dries.

Acrylics that are thinned enough can be poured without adding a pouring medium, but it's more of a challenge to achieve the unique effects a medium can produce.

There are many brands and types of pouring mediums for painters to choose from. Some are artist quality mediums made specifically for pour painting, and others are products that work similarly that can be used as alternatives to artist mediums.

ARTIST POURING MEDIUMS

Artist pouring mediums, also known as professional pouring mediums, are compatible with all the paint types listed in Chapter 3. The main reasons to choose a medium designed for pouring are consistent results and long-term durability. These mediums work well to optimize and enhance acrylic paint for pours, are archival quality, and won't crack or turn yellow over time.

A few brands available at many retail art supply stores and online include Chroma Atelier® Traditional Pouring Medium, Golden® Color Pouring Medium, Liquitex® Professional Pouring Medium, and Vallejo Pouring Medium.

Note: Available brands vary by country and location, so check with your local art supplier.

Other artist grade acrylic mediums that can be used for pouring include:

- Acrylic gloss medium
- Golden® GAC 800
- Golden® GAC 100

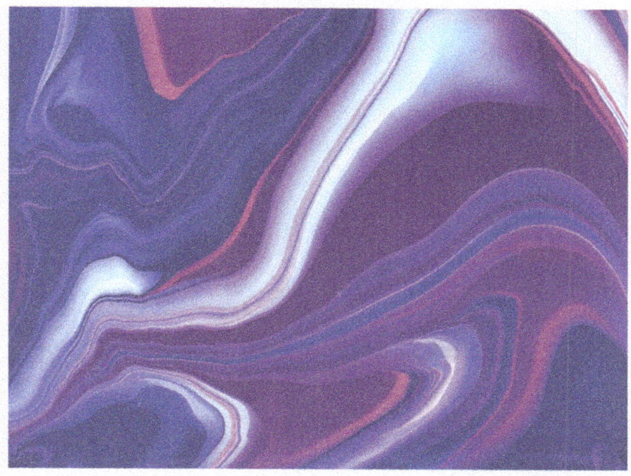

A pouring medium can give acrylic paint a marbleized appearance.

ALTERNATIVE MEDIUMS FOR POURING

The products below are options for pour painters seeking lower cost or alternative mediums for their pours. Like artist pouring mediums, they work with all the paint varieties mentioned in Chapter 3. Except where noted, they aren't archival quality.

PVA Glue - Multi-purpose PVA (polyvinyl acetate) glues such as Elmer's® Glue-All® (in the USA), and similar white PVA craft glues are less expensive than artist mediums. They're a good option for beginners and for practicing new techniques.

This type of glue can be purchased at arts & crafts supply stores, office supply stores, and online.

Bookbinding Glue - High-quality PVA bookbinding glues are comparable to artist pouring mediums in terms of durability. They cost more than the average PVA glue but won't crack or turn yellow over time. Glues such as Lineco® Neutral PVA Adhesive dry clear and are archival quality.

Floetrol® - Floetrol is a latex-based paint additive sold at paint and home improvement stores. This product can help cells form in the paint without an additional additive. It reduces the sheen of glossy paints and dries to a matte or satin finish depending on the paints it's combined with.

Tip: Be sure to have plenty of ventilation in your workspace when using this product.

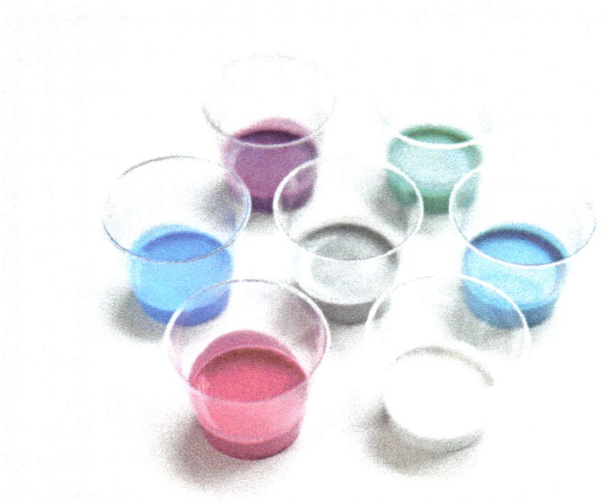

Acrylic paint and pouring medium mixtures

GLOSSY VS. MATTE POURING MEDIUMS

Glossy and matte pouring mediums work similarly despite their different finishes. Although choosing one is a matter of preference, here are a few things to consider.

- A glossy medium can make a painting dry to a high-shine finish, but the paint used can also influence the final sheen.
- Paintings produced with a matte finish pouring medium are easier to photograph because there's no glare from a glossy shine.
- No matter what medium you use, the sheen of a painting can be changed with a protective finish or coat of varnish.

MIXING AND MATCHING PAINT AND POURING MEDIUM BRANDS

Brands typically design their products to work together, so using the same brand of paint and pouring medium not only makes it easier to know the best ratio to start with but can give you confidence about the compatibility of the products. However, mixing and matching various brands can work just as well to create beautiful art.

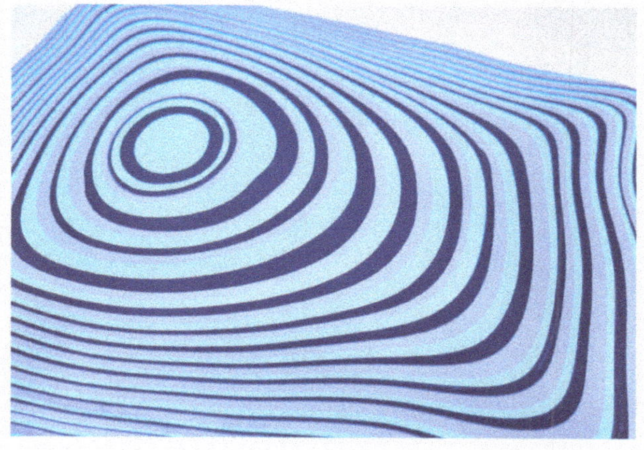

Paint puddles of acrylic paint and pouring medium

POURING MEDIUM TIPS

- In most instances, it takes more pouring medium than paint to complete a painting. I suggest starting with at least an 8 or 16 US fluid ounce bottle (237 or 473 mL). For reference, it takes roughly 3 to 5 US fluid ounces (89 to 148 mL) of pouring medium per 8 x 10-inch (20 x 25 cm) painting.
- If cost is an issue, consider starting with a white PVA multi-purpose glue.
- Experiment with a few mediums to find your favorite. While they can appear similar at first glance, there are usually some variances in how a painting turns out with each one.

- If you want your creations to last a long time, use an artist pouring medium combined with artist grade acrylic paints.
- It's possible to use more than one type or brand of pouring medium in a pour. If you discover you like certain qualities of specific mediums, they can be combined to create your ideal mix. If you decide to try this, I suggest noting the products and ratio used so you can repeat successful combinations.

paint additives for creating cells

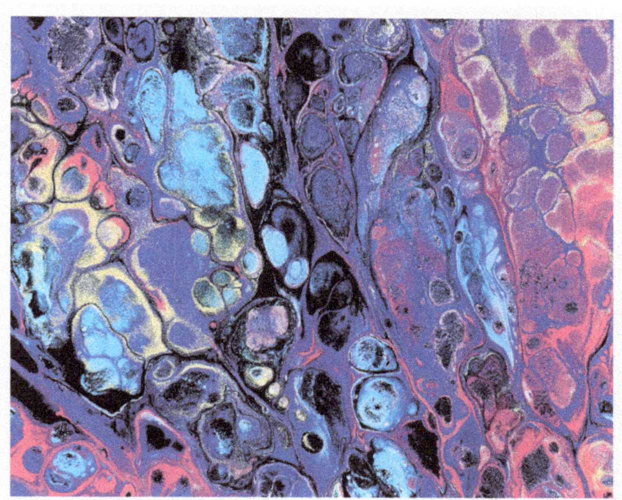

ANYONE FAMILIAR WITH POUR PAINTINGS HAS LIKELY SEEN POURS WITH fascinating circular and jewel-like shapes and patterns. Although these colorful "cells" sometimes develop organically due to air bubbles or variances in paint densities, several additives can make them more likely to occur. A few commonly used ones include:

- Silicone oils such as treadmill belt lubricants made with 100% silicone oil, or silicone oil made specifically for acrylic pour painting
- Dimethicone, a type of silicone used in some hair serums and various cosmetic products
- Isopropyl alcohol (91% or 70%)

Notes About Additives

- Additives should be put into paint mixtures just before pouring.
- If you'd like your painting to be archival quality, isopropyl alcohol is the best choice because the long-term durability of acrylic paints mixed with silicone or dimethicone is unknown.
- Oils used in acrylic pours leave a greasy residue on the painting's surface after it dries. If one plans to use a finishing spray or varnish on their completed painting, this must be removed. I've listed the steps for how to do this in Chapter 21.
- For further details about using additives to get cells in a painting, see Chapter 15 (Section 9) and Chapter 24 (Section 9).

pour painting surface options

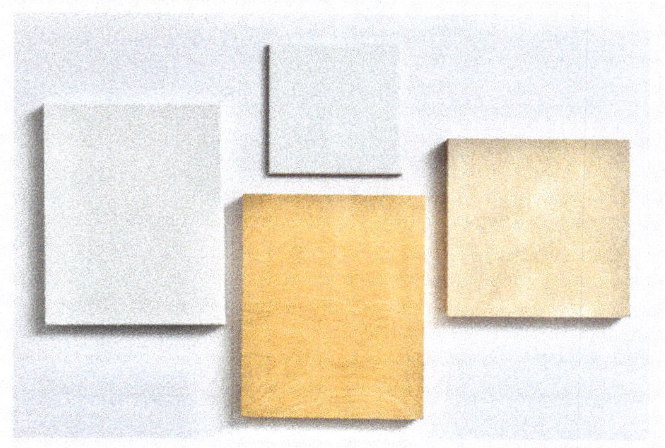

POUR PAINTERS HAVE MANY TRADITIONAL AND UNCONVENTIONAL SURFACE options to choose from. From canvases to rocks, here are a few possibilities to consider for your creations.

Stretched Canvases

Stretched canvases are available in an array of sizes, shapes, and qualities. They're sold individually or in cost-saving multi-packs, ideal for beginners who want plenty of canvases for practice.

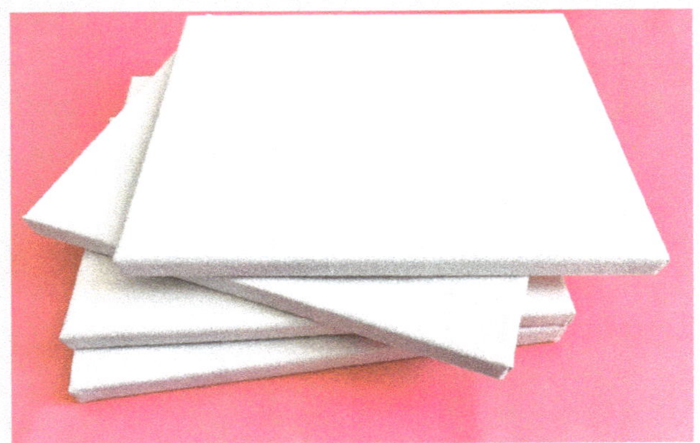

Student quality canvases are fine for getting started. As you become more experienced, consider using artist quality canvases made with heavier weight canvas and higher quality wood stretcher bars, which makes them well-suited for supporting the weight of a layer of paint and medium.

Canvases without staples on the sides, such as back-stapled or splined, can be displayed without a frame. They're also great for showing off the colorful paint drips on the edges of pour paintings.

When selecting canvases, choose ones that appear neatly constructed and have a tightly stretched surface. Avoid any that seem uneven, sag, or have ripples because this will negatively affect the painting.

Canvas Panels

The average canvas panel sold at art supply stores is made with a sheet of canvas surrounding a firm cardboard base. Since cardboard can warp beneath a layer of wet paint, these panels are better for practice or test paintings than those intended for display or sale.

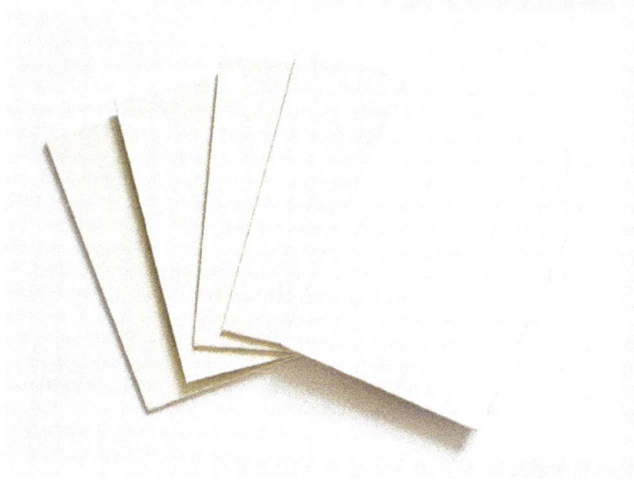

Canvas panels

Wood Artist Panels

Wood panels provide a smooth surface for poured paint. Like canvases, panels are sold in an assortment of types, sizes, and price points to suit every budget. Here are a few varieties you'll find at art supply stores.

Fiberboard Panels (MDF and HDF)

Fiberboard panels are engineered wood panels formed using heat and pressure to compress a wood fiber mixture. Two types of fiberboard panels used by painters are MDF panels (medium-density fiberboard) and HDF panels (high-density fiberboard). HDF is sometimes referred to as hardboard.

Besides a few variations in how these panels are made, the key differences between MDF and HDF are density and cost, with MDF panels being less dense and less expensive, which makes them popular with new painters.

Pre-Primed Wood Panels

There are many versions of pre-primed artist panels that can be used by professional artists or those who simply prefer the convenience of having a surface that's ready to paint on.

Solid Wood Panels

Solid wood artist painting panels made from woods such as birch, basswood, and maple are another option. These panels are well-sanded, so they have little to no wood texture, depending on the panel. They're available in student to professional qualities and price ranges, as well as flat and cradled varieties described below.

Flat or Cradled Wood Panels

Many varieties of wood panels are available in flat or cradled versions. A flat panel is a basic wood painting panel, and a cradled panel is a flat panel that's attached to a wood frame, giving it a deeper profile and making it less likely to warp. Another benefit of using a cradled wood panel is being able to display it without a frame.

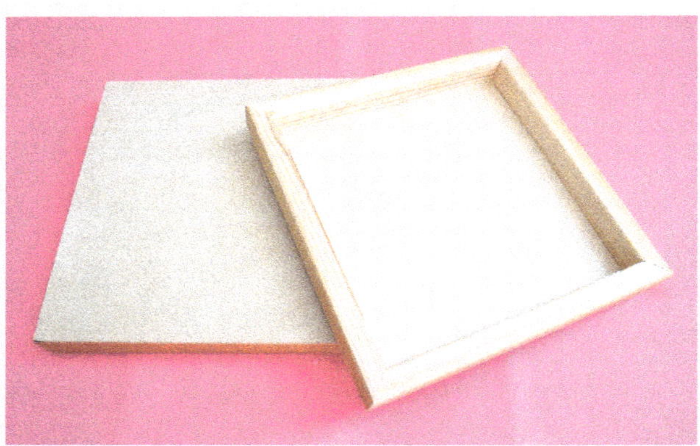

Cradled wood panels

Ceramic Tiles

White or ivory ceramic tiles are another option for acrylic pours. From 4 x 4-inch (10 x 10 cm) beverage coaster size tiles to much larger ones, they're inexpensive and sold at most flooring and home improvement stores. The only drawback to tiles is that they could break if dropped.

Yupo® Paper

Yupo is a smooth, waterproof paper made of 100% polypropylene. Unlike regular paper, wet paint won't cause it to curl, warp, or tear. Pour paintings on this type of paper can be framed like a watercolor painting or mounted on a wood panel or similar hard surface for display.

Canvas Pad

A canvas pad contains individual sheets of canvas that can be torn out to paint on. The sheets are thin and flexible, so it's a different experience than working with a firm painting surface. Chapter 16 (Section 5) offers tips for using canvas pad sheets and other flexible painting surfaces.

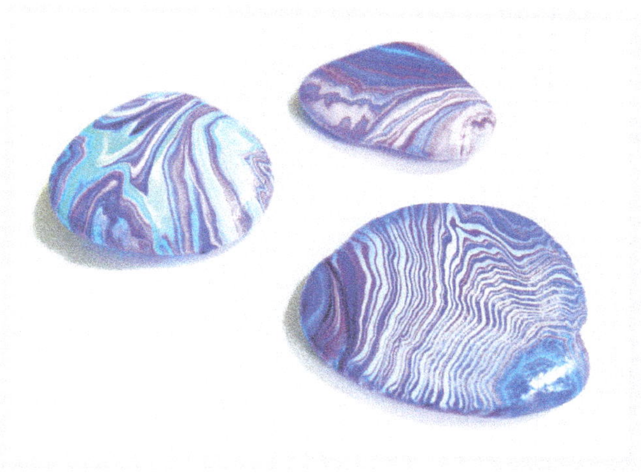

Pour painted rocks

Other Surfaces for Pouring

To explore even more surface options for your art, consider these ideas:

- Canvas paper (Canvas textured paper)
- Watercolor paper

- Mixed media paper
- Wood tabletop or other wood items
- Glass items or mirrors
- Ceramic items like vases, bowls, or photo frames
- Unwanted vinyl records
- Magnets
- Holiday ornaments
- Rocks

See Chapter 12 to learn how to prepare surfaces for pouring paint. Chapter 13 details how to gesso a canvas, and Chapter 14 lists the steps to seal and prime a wood panel.

CHAPTER 8

how to choose a workspace

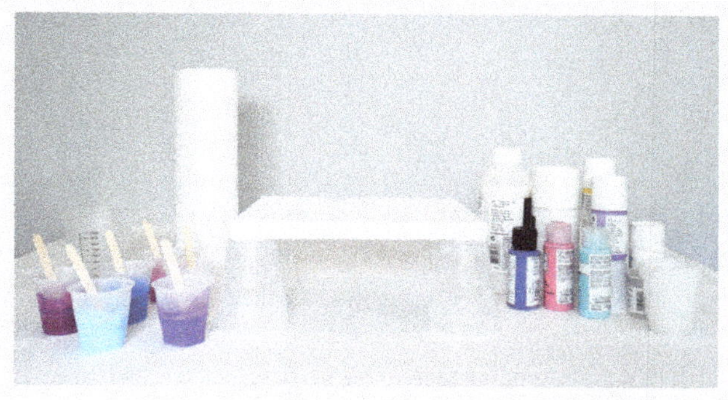

Choosing the right type of workspace can increase the chances of a successful painting. Since the artwork will stay wet for one to three days or more, a proper space can help prevent various issues that could affect the painting.

It's also important to note that this type of painting is quite messy. Unless you already have a specific arts & crafts area, you'll need to find a suitable location to work.

The list in this chapter includes considerations for where to do this project.

- A place where the painting can stay undisturbed until it's dry enough to move
- Well-lit, but not in direct sunlight
- Good ventilation
- A room temperature of approximately 60 to 80 degrees F (15 to 26 C)
- If possible, a climate-controlled space to prevent high humidity and temperature extremes, which can affect the painting's drying time
- A clean area without running fans that could blow dust particles onto the wet painting
- A location with a stable and level table or work surface to ensure the paint dries evenly
- An area with a floor that can be easily cleaned in case of paint spills
- If young children or pets are in the home, it's ideal to work in a room with a door that can be closed so they won't disturb the painting as it dries.

CHAPTER 9

pour painting safety tips

HERE ARE A FEW ESSENTIAL SAFETY TIPS AND SUGGESTIONS TO CONSIDER before, during, and after painting.

Ventilation

Not every painting product is non-toxic, so always work in an area with good ventilation. Read product labels for specific safety information about the paints, pouring mediums, additives, and varnishes used.

Disposable Gloves

Wearing disposable gloves while mixing paint, pouring, and during clean-up can keep hands clean and prevent them from coming in contact with painting products.

Multi-packs of latex, vinyl, or nitrile gloves in assorted sizes and lengths are easy to find at many stores and online. Choose nitrile gloves if you have a latex allergy.

Eye Protection

Since paints, mediums, or other liquid painting products can occasionally splash when opening bottles or mixing paint, consider wearing clear plastic safety glasses during the painting prep, pouring, and clean-up process. Look for these at house paint supply stores, hardware stores, or online.

Sanding Safety

When sanding canvases, wood, or other painting surfaces, it's advisable to wear safety goggles and a sanding or respirator mask.

Product Safety Information

For specific safety information about any paint, medium, varnish, or other products used in acrylic pouring, read product labels or visit the brand's website. These sites often have Safety Data Sheets (SDS), which provide details about each product.

Safely Storing Painting Supplies

Painting supplies such as paints, mediums, additives, and varnishes should be kept at an average room temperature, away from heat sources or sunlight, and always inaccessible to children or pets. Contact a poison control hotline or an appropriate medical provider immediately if any products are accidentally ingested.

Personalized Concerns

Anyone with health conditions, allergies, or concerns about using art products should consult a qualified healthcare provider before painting.

quick-start tutorial for first-time pour painters

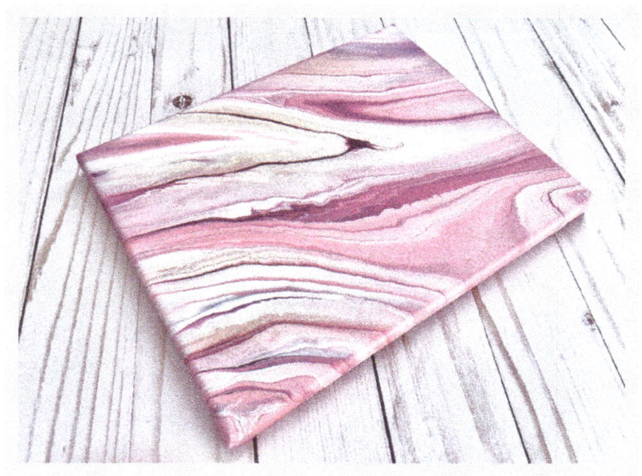

I DESIGNED THIS TUTORIAL FOR NEW PAINTERS WHO WANT TO CREATE RIGHT away with this fun art technique. It includes a short list of budget-friendly supplies, a few easy steps, and a pour painting recipe to take the guesswork out of how much paint and medium to use.

If you're not new to pouring or would prefer to start with my complete supply list and process, skip to Chapter 11.

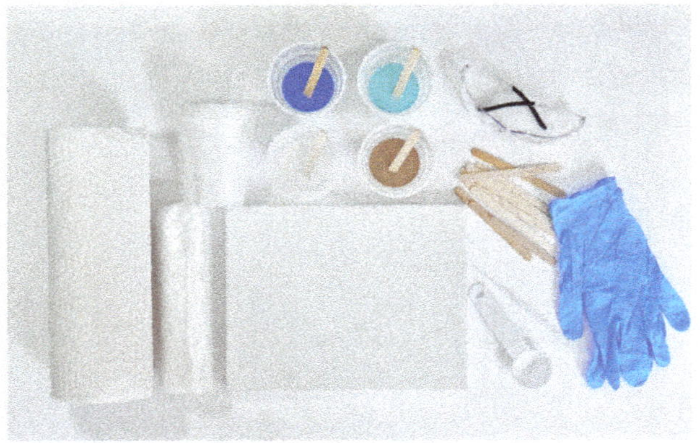

Supplies

The following items are available at arts & crafts supply stores, many discount stores, the craft section of some department stores, and online.

- One 8 x 10-inch (20 x 25 cm) stretched canvas or canvas panel
- Four bottles of craft acrylic paint (each a different color), at least 2 US fluid ounces each (59 mL) (See Chapter 4 for color combination ideas.)
- White PVA glue (such as Elmer's® Glue-All® in the USA), at least 4 US fluid ounces (118 mL)
- Nine plastic beverage cups, approximately 9 US fluid ounces (266 mL)
- Wood craft sticks or mixing sticks
- Plastic painting drop cloth or a large plastic trash bag
- Disposable gloves (latex, vinyl, or nitrile)
- Measuring spoon (You'll only need a US tablespoon or a 15 mL measuring spoon or cup for this recipe.)
- Plastic dropper or pipette for water
- Plastic safety glasses
- Apron and/or clothing you don't care if you get paint on
- Paper towels

Instructions

Step 1: Cover a stable, level table or similar surface with a plastic painting drop cloth or a large plastic trash bag.

Step 2: Holding the cap tight, shake each paint bottle before adding the measured amounts of paint and glue to each plastic cup, as listed below. Use a craft stick to scrape paint from the measuring spoon into the cups.

Tip: Add the glue first for easier mixing.

Cup 1

- 2 tablespoons (30 mL) of glue
- 1 tablespoon (15 mL) of paint color one

Cup 2

- 2 tablespoons (30 mL) of glue
- 1 tablespoon (15 mL) of paint color two

Cup 3

- 2 tablespoons (30 mL) of glue
- 1 tablespoon (15 mL) of paint color three

Cup 4

- 2 tablespoons (30 mL) of glue
- 1 tablespoon (15 mL) of paint color four

Cup 5

- Add some water to this cup to use in the next step.

Step 3: Use a craft stick to blend the paint and glue into a smooth, uniform color and consistency. Slow mixing will reduce the number of air bubbles that form.

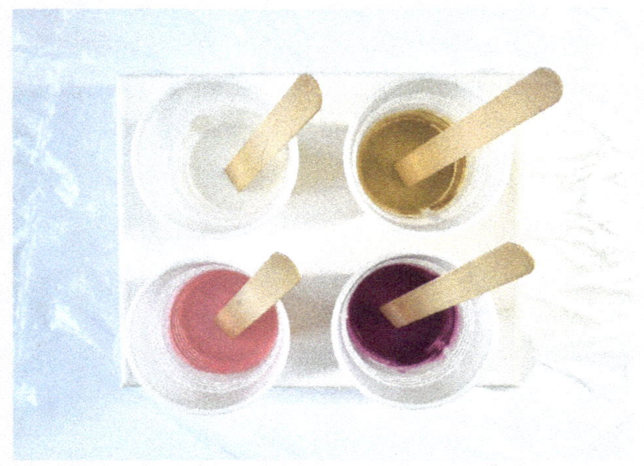

Cups of craft acrylic paint and glue mixture

The ideal consistency for paint pouring is like warm honey or chocolate syrup. It should flow smoothly and easily without being watery.

Use a plastic pipette or dropper to add a small amount of water to the paint/glue mixture. Do this in small increments and gently re-stir until the correct consistency is reached.

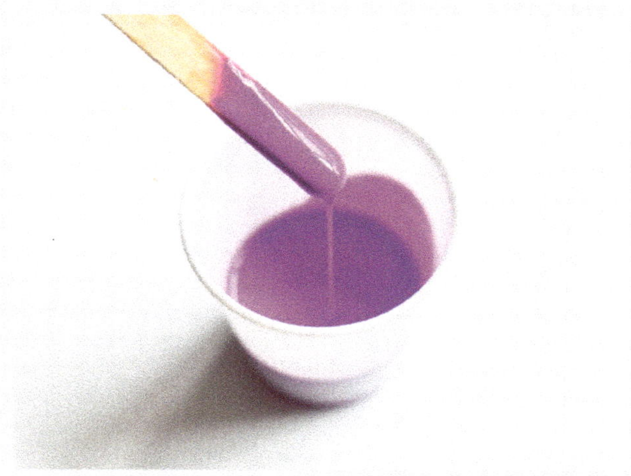

At the correct consistency, the paint and glue mixture should drip
from the craft stick in a steady stream and flatten into the rest of the
paint within a second.

Tip: Try to limit the amount of water added to less than 20 to 30% of the total mixture volume to prevent paint cracking.

If air bubbles are in the paint cups after mixing is complete, let them sit for about twenty minutes or until most of the bubbles have dissipated.

Step 4: Place the stretched canvas on four upside down plastic beverage cups on the covered surface to keep it raised while pouring.

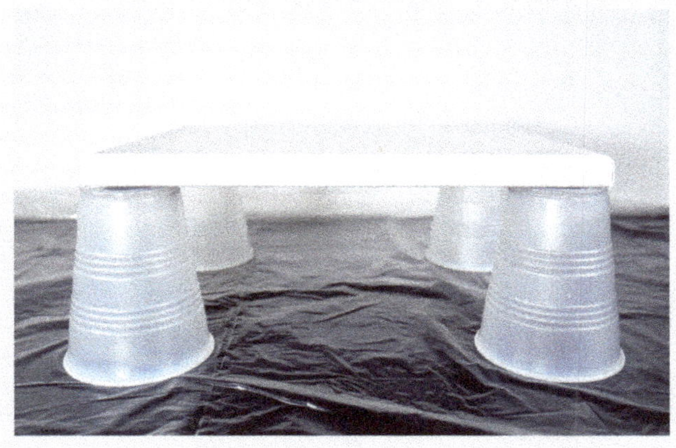

Canvas raised on beverage cups

Note: If using a canvas panel, place it directly onto the covered surface rather than on cups to prevent warping.

Step 5: Pour the paint from each cup onto the canvas in any way you like until the canvas is mostly covered.

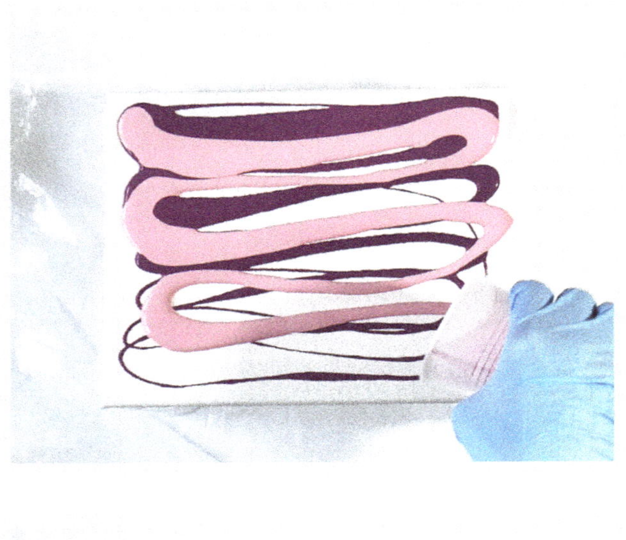

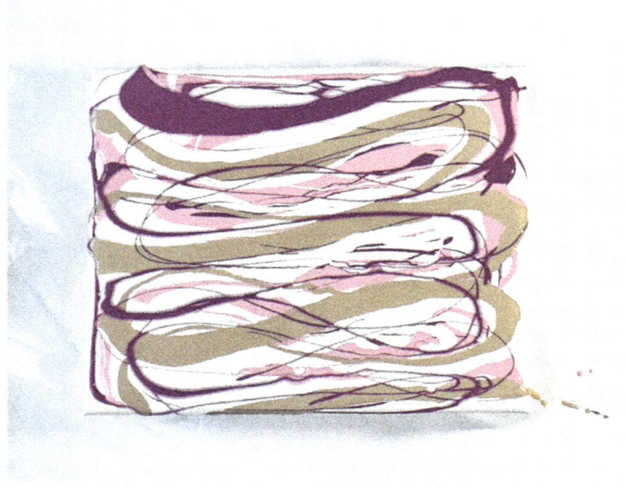

Step 6: Carefully pick up the canvas and tilt it slowly in different directions to let the paint move around and blend into interesting abstract designs.

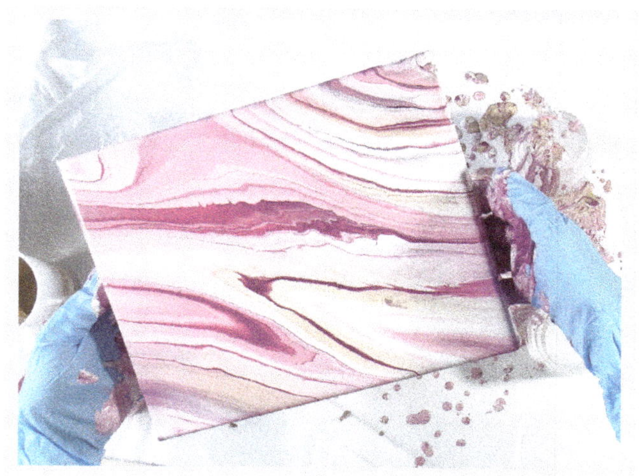

Tilting the canvas to blend the paint

Step 7: Once the canvas is thoroughly and evenly covered with paint, and you're happy with how the painting looks, place it squarely on the four beverage cups to dry.

Tip: A canvas panel should be placed on a paint-free section of the drop cloth or table covering, so it's not sitting in a puddle of paint as it dries.

Step 8: Give the painting approximately two to four days to dry before touching or moving it. Exact drying times will vary based on the environmental conditions in your workspace and the type of paints and glue used.

Notes:

If the paint mixtures seem too thick, add a small amount of additional water and slowly re-stir. If they seem too thin, add a small amount of extra paint and re-stir. A good paint consistency prevents various issues and ensures that there will be a sufficient amount of color to cover the entire canvas.

This tutorial uses the Traditional Pour Technique, which is one of the easiest for new painters. See Chapter 16 (pp. 92-94) for expanded instructions for this technique.

This recipe works with craft acrylic paint and white PVA glue; however, any acrylic paint (craft, student, or professional) and pouring medium can be used. Adjustments to the paint-to-medium ratio and amount of water might be needed to get the paint mixture to an optimal consistency. Like everything with pour painting, experiment!

pour painting supplies: essential & optional items

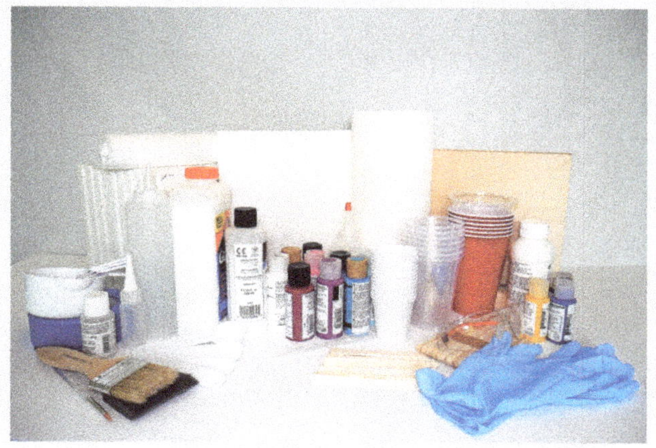

Once you're familiar with the options for paints, pouring medium, additives, and surfaces, you're likely wondering what other materials you'll need. In this chapter, you'll find a list of must-have supplies and optional ones to consider as you continue to explore this style of painting. All the items here are mentioned in this book, so if you haven't heard of them yet, you will find them in upcoming chapters.

The art-related supplies are sold at art supply stores and online. The others can be found at most discount stores and home improvement stores.

I suggest starting with items on the Essential Supplies list and adding optional supplies as needed. If you're a cost-conscious painter, you'll find tips for minimizing supply costs at the end of this chapter.

ESSENTIAL SUPPLIES

- Acrylic paints (fluid, liquid, soft body, high flow, or craft acrylics) in at least three or four colors
- Bottle of pouring medium, at least 8 to 16 US fluid ounces (237 to 473 mL)
- Cell-producing paint additive (Only if you want a painting with cells)
- Painting surfaces, such as stretched canvases or wood panels
- Gesso, small bottle or container to prime canvases or wood panels
- Wide, flat paintbrush or foam brush for gesso application, 2 to 3 inches wide (5 to 7.6 cm)
- Acrylic gloss medium or Golden® GAC 100 (If using unprimed wood panels)
- Wide, flat paintbrush to apply a sealer to a wood panel, 2 to 3 inches wide (5 to 7.6 cm) (If using unprimed wood panels)
- 2 or 3 small, shallow dishes, bowls, or containers for gesso, sealer, or varnish
- Set of measuring spoons and cups
- Pack of plastic beverage cups for paint mixing and pouring in two sizes: approximately 3 to 5 US fluid ounces (89 to 148 mL) and 9 to 16 US fluid ounces (266 to 473 mL)
- Plastic food wrap to cover paint cups
- Medium size rubber bands to secure food wrap
- Pack of wood, plastic, or silicone-coated craft/mixing sticks for mixing paint

- Four empty metal food cans (soup size or smaller), a wire cooling rack, or plastic beverage cups to elevate the canvas/painting surface
- Plastic painting drop cloth or plastic sheeting to protect the table/work area
- Apron to protect clothing
- Pack of disposable gloves (vinyl, latex, or nitrile)
- Plastic safety glasses
- Paper towels
- Mild liquid dish soap
- Microfiber or other lint-free cloth

OPTIONAL SUPPLIES

The supplies on these lists can be used for various aspects of pour painting, from start to finish.

Before Painting

- Color wheel
- Plastic pipettes to add water or paint additives to paint mixtures
- Small level to ensure the painting surface is even
- Sandpaper (#220 grit) to smooth the canvas after gesso application
- Sanding mask (if sanding painting surfaces)
- Safety goggles (if sanding painting surfaces)
- Painter's tape to protect the back of the painting
- Aluminum foil to protect the back of the painting
- Parchment paper or a large silicone craft mat to place beneath the painting
- Disposable, flat-bottom aluminum cookie or baking pan to contain paint drippings
- Small canvas panels for test paintings
- Split cup for dirty pours

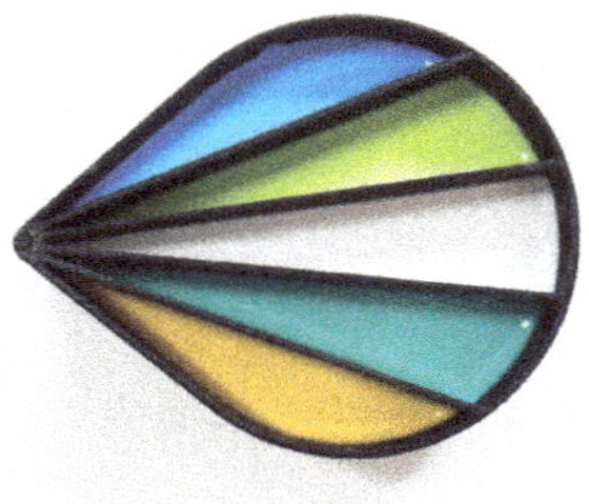

A split cup with five channels for paint

During Painting

- Palette knife (plastic or metal) to blend paint or make designs
- Plastic squeeze bottles to pour paint or to store paint mixtures
- Toothpicks or sewing pins to pop air bubbles
- Items to make designs or move wet paint: drinking straws or coffee stirrers, plastic forks, toothpicks, string, beaded curtain pull chain for drapery, wide-tooth hair comb, paintbrushes, spackle knife, hair dryer or mini air blower

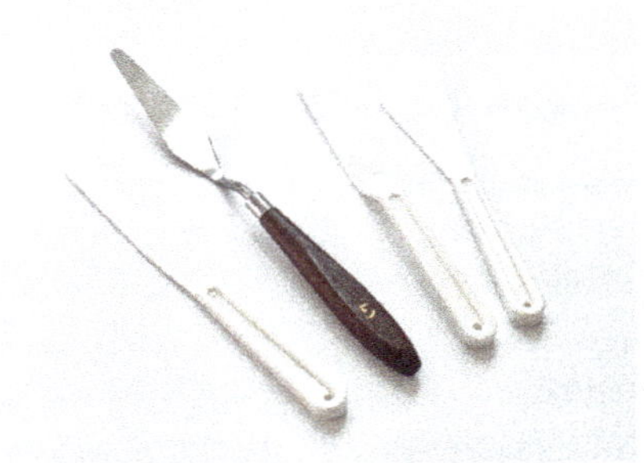

Assorted palette knives

Painting Edge Touch-Ups

- Small plastic paint palette or a palette paper pad
- Small synthetic bristle artist paintbrush (round or filbert)

Protecting the Finished Painting

- Varnish of choice
- Varnish brush (for brush-on varnishes)

For Removing Silicone or Other Oils Before Varnishing (If Applicable)

- Disposable cookie or cake pan or large towel to cover the work area
- Corn starch
- Soft cloth or soft sponge
- Mild liquid dish soap

Painting Display

- Frame to display painting
- Picture hanging kit

Miscellaneous

- Artist brush soap for paintbrush cleaning
- Masking tape and/or clear tape for miscellaneous purposes
- Scissors for miscellaneous purposes
- Pumice grain bar soap
- Plastic container with handles to move and store painting supplies

WAYS TO LOWER SUPPLY COSTS

It's possible to keep costs to a minimum and have everything you need to paint. Before buying supplies, gather any you already have at home. Many items on the Essential Supplies list, such as stretched canvases, painting drop cloths, plastic cups, and wood craft sticks, can be purchased inexpensively at many discount stores.

For further savings, search for sale-priced craft, student, or artist acrylics at arts & crafts stores and opt for a multi-purpose white PVA glue or Floetrol® as a lower-cost alternative to an artist pouring medium.

CHAPTER 12

painting surface prep

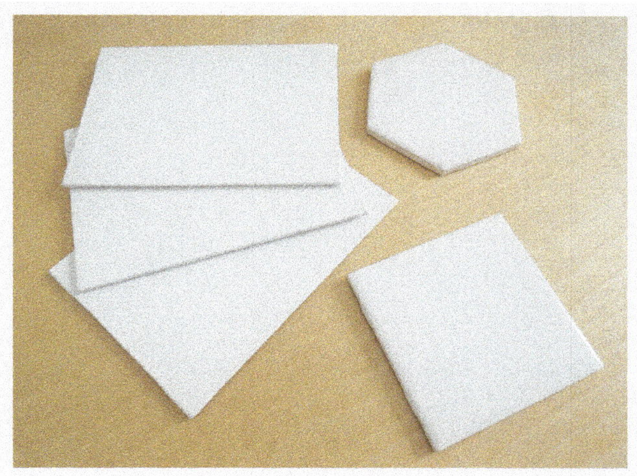

A PROPERLY PREPARED SURFACE INCREASES THE CHANCES OF A PAINTING'S success. Here are details about how to get various surface types pour-ready.

Stretched Canvases and Canvas Panels

It's best to prime a new canvas or canvas panel with gesso a day prior to starting a painting. If this process is unfamiliar to you, Chapter 13 provides step-by-step instructions.

Wood Artist Panels

Unless a wood panel is labeled as "pre-primed" and ready to paint on, it should be sealed and primed to prevent warping and paint discoloration. See Chapter 14 to learn how to do this.

Ceramic Tiles

Unglazed tiles - Seal a clean, dry tile with a layer of acrylic gloss medium. Allow this to dry before applying a coat of gesso.

Glazed (shiny) tiles - Clean the tile with isopropyl alcohol on a paper towel or lint-free cloth just before pouring. This will remove dirt, dust, or fingerprints that could prevent the paint from adhering. It's best to skip the gesso with glazed tiles because it could leave flakes in the wet paint.

Canvas Pad Sheets

No special surface prep is needed; however, adding a coat of gesso can smooth the surface and give the paint a better grip.

Yupo® Paper

This type of paper can be used as is.

Wood Tabletop or Other Wood Items

Assuming the item is in relatively good condition, clean it with wood soap to remove dust and dirt, and wait about a week for it to fully dry. Next, sand the painting surface areas with #150 or #220 grit sandpaper. After brushing off the dust, follow the steps for sealing and priming a wood panel as listed in Chapter 14.

Glass Items

Thoroughly clean the item and let it dry. To remove fingerprints, wipe the entire surface with isopropyl alcohol on a paper towel or lint-free cloth before pouring.

Ceramic Items

Prepare ceramic items like vases, bowls, and picture frames the same way as ceramic tiles.

Rocks

Wash rocks outdoors or in a bucket to prevent dirt or sand sediment from clogging a sink drain. Rinse well and give them a few days to dry. Next, brush on a coat of acrylic gloss medium or Golden® GAC 100 and let this dry before adding a coat of gesso.

Surface Prep Safety Tip

Before sanding any painting surface, please review "Sanding Safety" in Chapter 9.

how to prepare a canvas

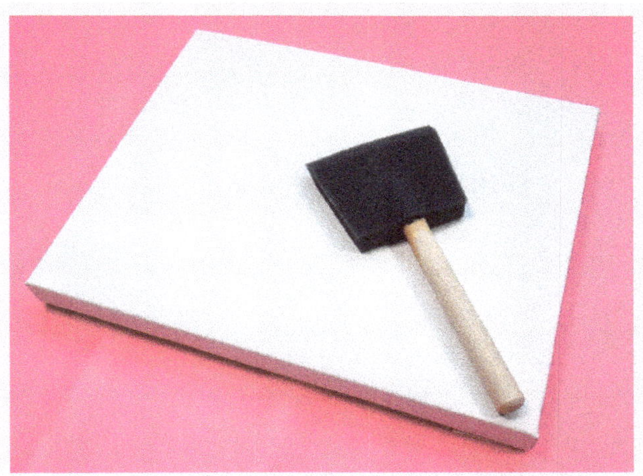

To get a canvas ready for pouring, a coat of gesso (an acrylic primer) should be applied to the surface and sides. Gesso helps smooth the texture of the canvas and enables the paint and pouring medium to adhere more easily.

Some brands of gesso require just a single coat, while others take two. It takes about a day for each coat to dry, so plan time to prime the canvas before starting a project.

If you're new to priming a canvas, this chapter provides a list of supplies and application steps, answers to a few commonly asked questions about gesso, and instructions for keeping the back of the canvas clean while painting.

Supplies

- Stretched canvas or canvas panel
- Bottle or container of white gesso
- Wide, flat paintbrush or foam brush, 2 to 3 inches (5 to 7.6 cm) wide for smaller canvases and 4 inches (10 cm) or more for larger ones
- Small, shallow dish or bowl for gesso
- Small container of water
- Two to four small objects to raise the canvas, such as small empty cans or food container lids
- Microfiber or other lint-free cloth
- Covering for the table (plastic sheeting, towel, or silicone craft mat)
- Paper towels or paint rag for clean-up

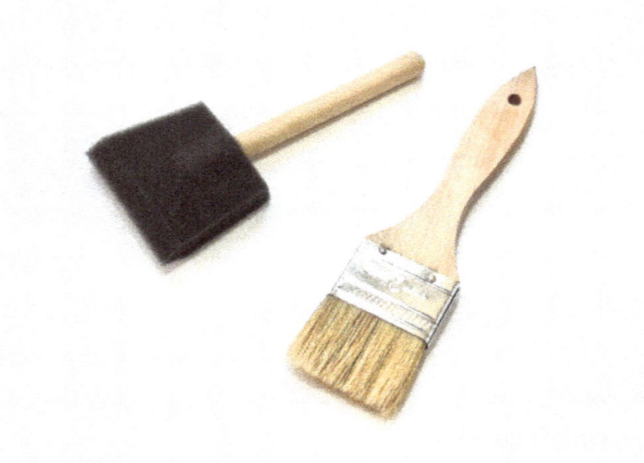

Brush options for applying gesso

Instructions

Step 1: Use a clean, dry microfiber or other lint-free cloth to clean the canvas of dust or dirt before starting.

Step 2: Cover the table/work area and have the empty cans or food container lids nearby to keep the canvas raised after applying the gesso.

Step 3: Pour a small amount of gesso into a shallow dish or bowl.

Step 4: Dampen the paintbrush or foam brush with water. Wipe off any excess on a paper towel. The brush should be slightly damp but not wet.

Step 5: Use the brush to apply a thin, even coat of gesso over the entire canvas and sides. Brush in one direction, either horizontally or vertically.

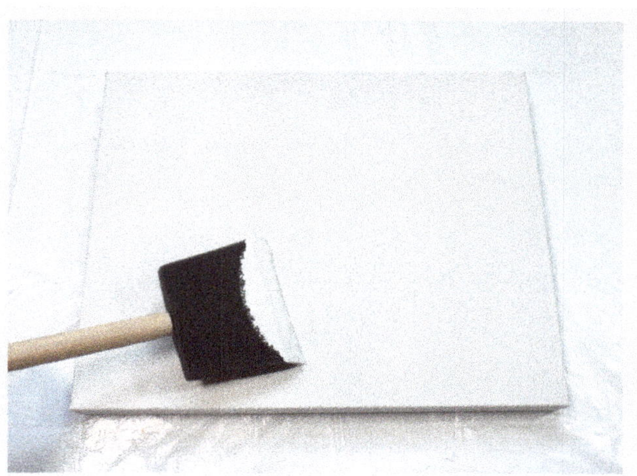

Applying gesso with a foam brush

Step 6: When finished, place the canvas on a raised surface and let it dry for about a day.

If the brand of gesso you're using requires two coats, repeat Steps 1 through 6 for a second coat, applying the gesso in the opposite direction as the first application.

Clean-Up

If there's leftover gesso in the dish, it can be poured back into the bottle if this is done before it starts to dry.

Wipe excess gesso from the brush before washing it well with a mild liquid dish soap or an artist brush soap and water. Rinse the brush and place it on a towel to dry.

Sand the Canvas (Optional)

For the smoothest painting surface, lightly sand the canvas with a very fine grit sandpaper (#220) after each coat of gesso is dry. It's best to wear safety goggles and a sanding or respirator mask during this process. Use a cloth to wipe the dust from the canvas after each sanding and before painting.

Gesso Questions & Answers

What kind of gesso should I buy and how much will I need?

Gesso is sold in white, black, clear, and an assortment of colors. White is the most commonly used for canvases, but this is a matter of preference. A colored gesso will be visible if using transparent or translucent acrylic paints or inks.

It only takes a little gesso to prime small or medium size canvases, so a 4 to 8 US fluid ounce bottle (118 to 237 mL) or container should be plenty to start with.

Tip: Use an artist quality gesso for pour painting because lesser quality ones might leave flakes in the wet paint.

Is it necessary to gesso a canvas labeled as "pre-primed"?

Applying a coat or two of gesso will help the paint and pouring medium stick to the canvas as it's moved around to make the paint flow. I use it even with pre-primed canvases, but it's OK to skip if you're painting just for fun and your paintings turn out well without it.

How to Protect the Back of the Canvas

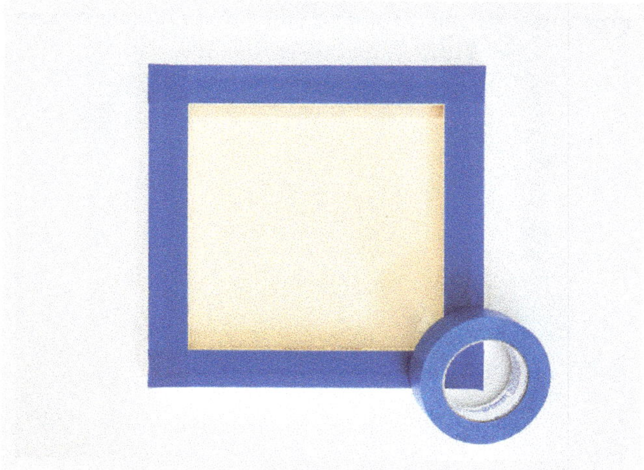

Once the gesso is dry, the back of the canvas can be covered to prevent it from getting coated with paint. This step is optional, but if you want to do it, here's how.

Supplies

- Stretched canvas
- Painter's tape
- Aluminum foil (Optional)

Instructions

Step 1: Cover the wood bars on the back of the canvas with painter's tape. Leave the edges of the canvas (sides) uncovered so the paint can drip down and cover them.

Optional: Place a piece of aluminum foil flat against the back of the canvas and tape the edges to secure it.

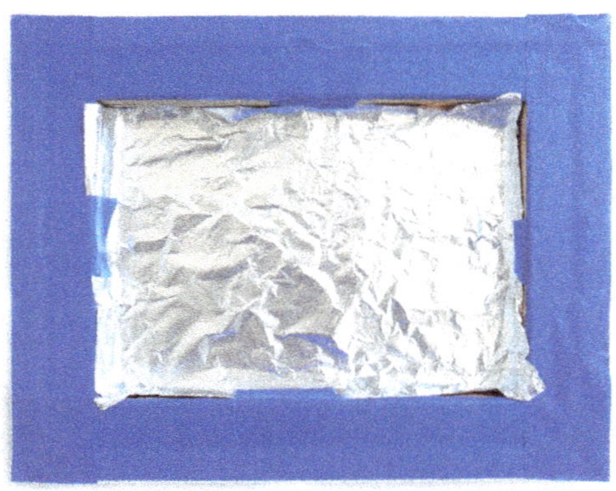

The painter's tape can be removed after the painting has had a few days to dry. This type of tape is easy to peel off and won't damage the canvas but be careful not to pull the paint film.

The back of a wood panel can be covered in the same way.

how to prepare a wood panel

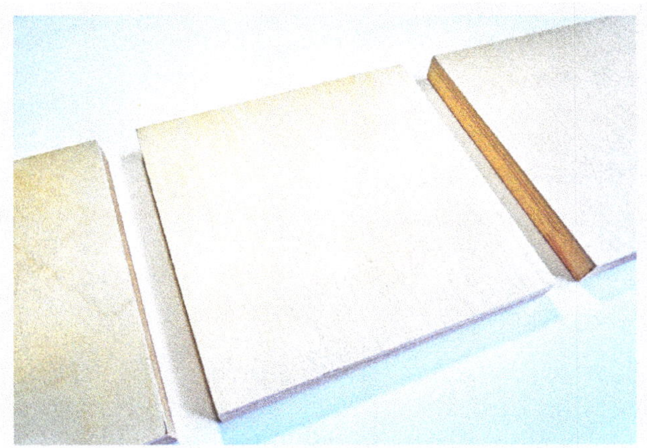

TAKING THE TIME TO SEAL AND PRIME A WOOD PANEL WILL PREVENT problems like warping and paint discoloration. This easy two-part process includes sealing the panel to keep moisture out and priming it with gesso.

Supplies

- Clean, dry wood panel
- Sealer options: Acrylic gloss medium or Golden® GAC 100
- Wide, flat paintbrush, 2 to 3 inches (5 to 7.6 cm) wide for smaller panels or 4 inches (10 cm) wide or more for larger ones
- Small, shallow dish or bowl for sealer
- Clean craft stick or similar item to stir sealer
- Two to four small objects to raise the panel from the table, such as small empty cans or food container lids
- Microfiber or other lint-free cloth
- A covering for the table (towel, plastic sheeting, or silicone craft mat)
- Paper towels or paint rag for clean-up

Instructions

Step 1: Use a clean, dry microfiber or other lint-free cloth to clean any dust or dirt from the panel before starting.

Step 2: Cover the table/work area and have the empty cans or food container lids nearby to keep the panel raised after applying the sealer. This will prevent it from sticking to the table.

Step 3: Give the sealer a light stir with a clean craft stick or stirrer before pouring some into a dish or bowl.

Step 4: Brush an even coat of sealer onto the panel in neat, horizontal strokes. Cover the sides, too, for the best protection.

Step 5: When finished, place the panel on a raised surface and allow this layer to fully dry before repeating Steps 1 through 4 to apply a second coat, brushing the sealer in the opposite direction as the first coat.

Note: Check the product label for drying time.

Step 6: Once the front and sides of the panel are fully dry, repeat Steps 1 through 5 to seal the back of the panel.

Step 7: Once the entire panel is dry, the front and sides can be primed with gesso, as described in Chapter 13.

Clean-Up

The sealers listed in this chapter are water-soluble. After wiping the brush clean on a paper towel or paint rag, wash it with a mild liquid dish soap or an artist brush soap and water before placing it on a towel to dry.

how to mix paints and pouring medium

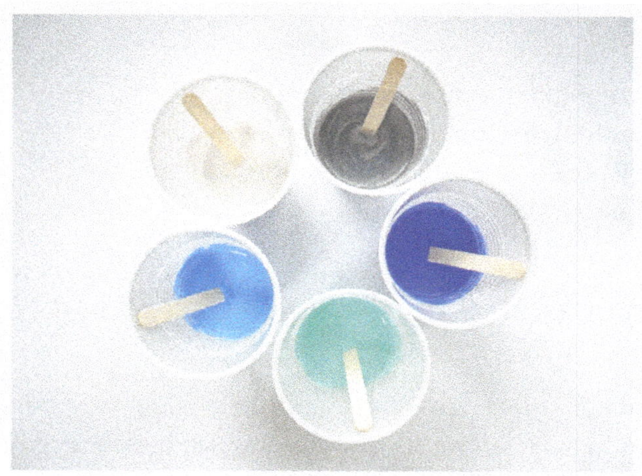

READY TO MIX YOUR PAINT? THIS CHAPTER GOES IN-DEPTH INTO PREPARING acrylic paint for pouring, from set-up to paint that's ready to pour.

1. SETTING UP AND SUPPLIES NEEDED

To prepare the paint for your pour, you'll need at least two to four paint colors that look good together, the pouring medium of your choice, and a mixing cup for each color. Cups of approximately 3 to 5 US fluid ounces (89 to 148 mL) are ideal for small and medium size paintings.

Tip: If you plan to try one of the pouring techniques in Chapter 16, refer to the specific technique for the suggested number of colors for that pour type.

You'll also need:

- Craft or mixing sticks to mix paint
- Measuring spoons and/or measuring cups
- Disposable gloves
- Plastic safety glasses
- Paper towels
- A covering for the table/work area
- Paint additive (Optional)
- Plastic pipette to add water (If needed)
- Cup with water (If needed)

2. HOW MUCH PAINT AND POURING MEDIUM IS NEEDED FOR A SPECIFIC PAINTING SIZE

Pour painting requires lots of paint, so it's vital to have enough mixed and ready before starting a painting. Besides having enough to fully cover the canvas or painting surface, it's beneficial to have extra in case too much flows over the sides or to make quick corrections while the paint is still wet.

Some pouring techniques require more paint than others, and canvases with deep profiles (thick edges) need more paint if you'd like the paint to cover the sides and have the option of displaying the artwork without a frame.

Bottom line: It's better to have leftover paint for another painting than not enough to complete the current one.

Here's the formula I use to estimate the total volume of paint and medium needed for a specific painting size.

It takes about **.07 US fluid ounces** of total paint/pouring medium mixture of the proper consistency (described in Section 3) per square inch of canvas/painting surface. For example, if using an 8 x 10-inch (20 x 25 cm) canvas:

8 x 10 = 80 square inches of painting surface

.07 x 80 = 5.6 US fluid ounces (166 mL) of paint/pouring medium mixture

Using this formula, here's how much paint/pouring medium mixture is suggested for several painting surface sizes.

5 x 7-inch (13 x 18 cm)	–	2.45 fluid ounces (72.5 mL)
6 x 6-inch (15.2 x 15.2 cm)	–	2.5 fluid ounces (74 mL)
8 x 8-inch (20 x 20 cm)	–	4.5 fluid ounces (133 mL)
8 x 10-inch (20 x 25 cm)	–	5.6 fluid ounces (166 mL)
11 x 14-inch (28 x 36 cm)	–	10.8 fluid ounces (319 mL)
16 x 20-inch (40 x 51 cm)	–	22.4 fluid ounces (662 mL)

Amounts are in US fluid ounces.

If this formula leaves too much extra paint, try using .05 or .06 per square inch rather than .07 to multiply with your surface area. If it's not enough, increase the number to .08.

You can also save leftover paint for a future project or use it to make an additional painting. I like to keep a few 4 x 4-inch (10 x 10 cm) ceramic tiles on hand to make small paintings or beverage coasters with extra paint. Chapter 17 lists the steps for how to do this.

Tip: Flat surfaces like Yupo® paper, canvas pad sheets, canvas panels, mixed media or watercolor paper, and glass typically require less paint than thicker, textured surfaces like stretched canvases.

3. OPTIMAL PAINT MIXTURE CONSISTENCY

The right paint mixture consistency is a key component of a successful pour painting. It should resemble warm honey or chocolate syrup, slightly thicker than a liquid coffee creamer but not watery. If you lift the mixing stick from the paint cup, the paint should drip down in a steady stream and then flatten into the rest of the paint in the cup within a second.

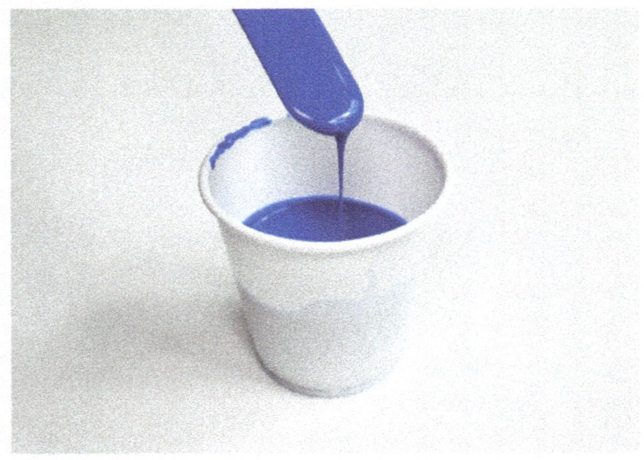

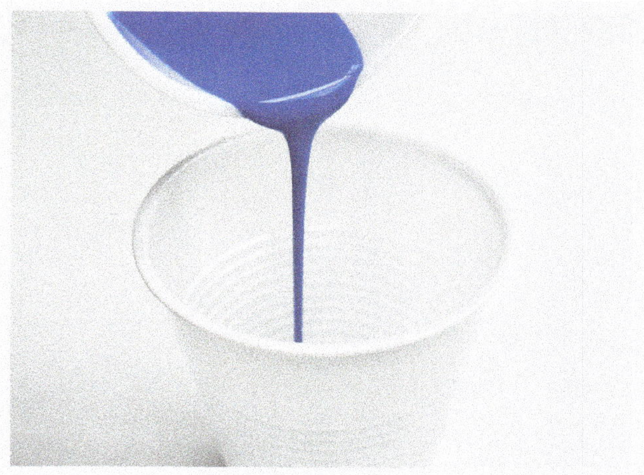

Some pouring techniques require a slightly thicker or thinner paint consistency, but the one described here works for most methods popular with beginners, including those you'll find in this book.

Many common pour painting problems can be prevented by ensuring the paint is at a proper consistency. Thin mixtures can spill over the edges too quickly and make the painting more challenging to complete or cause the colors to blend too much and appear muddy. Thick paint is slow to move across the painting surface, takes longer to dry, and may cause a lumpy finish. It's also more likely to crack or craze as the painting dries. Sometimes, artwork turns out well with a less-than-ideal paint consistency, but it's best to avoid this problem.

Getting the paint to a good consistency can take practice. Low viscosity acrylic paints combined with a good quality pouring medium is the easiest combination to work with because these products are at a ready-to-pour consistency right out of the bottle. If you have another type of acrylic paint, don't worry. As you'll learn in this chapter, it's possible to make every type of acrylics workable for pouring.

4. HOW TO CORRECT PAINT CONSISTENCY ISSUES

If the paint mixture consistency isn't right, here's how to fix it.

Too thin or watery: Stir in some additional paint in small increments until the consistency improves.

Too thick: Add a small amount of additional pouring medium or a little water. Stir and repeat as needed.

5. PAINT-TO-POURING MEDIUM RATIOS

Since there are many types, viscosities, and brands of acrylic paints, pouring mediums, and combinations thereof, there's not a single paint-to-pouring medium ratio that's right for every situation. One of the easiest ways for beginners to figure out the best ratio is to see if the bottle of pouring medium suggests one. If this information isn't on the bottle, check the product's page on the manufacturer's website. Suggested starting ratios work best when using the same brand of paints and pouring medium. Mixing and matching various products works too, but it can take some experimentation to find the right amounts.

General Guidelines for How Much Paint vs. Pouring Medium to Use

It typically takes more craft acrylic paint to match the color intensity as an artist grade one. For example, craft acrylics are usually mixed with a pouring medium at a 1:2 ratio, whereas some artist grade products suggest starting with a 1:10 paint-to-pouring medium ratio.

Painters may also wish to adjust the ratio depending on how saturated they want their colors to be, increasing the amount of paint for stronger color intensity and reducing it for more muted hues.

As you become familiar with various products, it becomes easier to estimate how much to use, and you won't need to follow a recipe unless you choose to.

If you're unsure what ratio to use, below are my suggested starting ratios for several types of acrylic paints and pouring mediums. These amounts should only be considered a general guide. Adjustments may be necessary depending on your specific paints and pouring medium and your preferences.

Craft Acrylic Paint Combined with White PVA Glue or Other Pouring Medium

1:2 Paint-to-Glue or Pouring Medium Ratio

- 1 Part Craft Acrylic Paint
- 2 Parts Glue or Pouring Medium

If needed, add water in small increments and gently blend until the mixture reaches an optimal consistency, as described in Section 3 of this chapter.

For stronger color intensity, try:

1:1 Paint-to-Glue or Pouring Medium Ratio

- 1 Part Craft Acrylic Paint
- 1 Part Glue or Pouring Medium

If needed, add water in small increments and gently blend until the mixture reaches an optimal consistency, as described in Section 3 of this chapter.

Artist Grade Liquid, Fluid, or Soft Body Acrylic Paints and Pouring Medium

1:10 Paint-to-Pouring Medium Ratio

- 1 Part Acrylic Paint
- 10 Parts Pouring Medium

If the colors aren't strong enough with a 1:10 ratio, try:

1:5 Paint-to-Pouring Medium Ratio

- 1 Part Acrylic Paint
- 5 Parts Pouring Medium

Medium Viscosity Acrylic Paint and Pouring Medium

1:3 Paint-to-Pouring Medium Ratio

- 1 Part Acrylic Paint
- 3 Parts Pouring Medium

If the mixture is too thick, add some additional pouring medium or a small amount of water to reach the right consistency.

High Flow Acrylic Paint and Pouring Medium

1:10 Paint-to-Pouring Medium Ratio

- 1 Part Acrylic Paint
- 10 Parts Pouring Medium

For more intense colors, try:

1:5 Paint-to-Pouring Medium Ratio

- 1 Part Acrylic Paint
- 5 Parts Pouring Medium

Acrylic Inks and Pouring Medium

Acrylic inks usually come in bottles with droppers. Instead of using a specific ratio, try adding several drops of ink to each small mixing cup with pouring medium. Thoroughly blend the mixture, and if necessary, continue adding drops and stirring until you reach your desired color intensity.

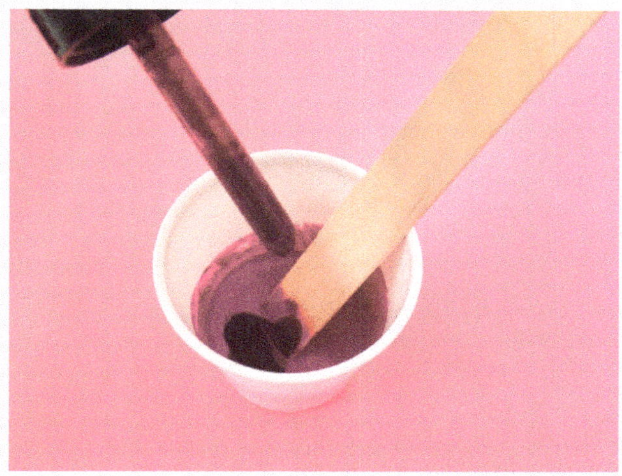

Adding acrylic ink to pouring medium

6. HOW TO MIX PAINT AND POURING MEDIUM

Most bottles of acrylic paint and acrylic ink should be shaken before using them. Some paints might come out of the bottle watery because of ingredient separation. Just be sure to hold the cap while shaking bottles.

Most pouring mediums don't need to be shaken. However, there are some exceptions, such as with Floetrol®. Glue sometimes separates if it hasn't been used in a while, so the bottle should be moved around for the ingredients to recombine. It's best to do this a few hours before paint mixing in case air bubbles form in the glue.

With all painting products, follow the instructions on the bottle for the best results.

Add the pouring medium to the mixing cup, followed by the paint. Next, use a craft or mixing stick to blend the mixture slowly and completely until it appears smooth and is one solid color. Slow mixing can help prevent air bubbles. Avoid whisking paint because it will create lots of tiny bubbles.

7. ADDING WATER TO PAINT MIXTURES

Water is sometimes added to paint and pouring medium mixtures to create an optimal consistency. This is more common when using thicker paints like craft acrylics, medium body acrylics, or heavy body acrylics.

If using a high-quality pouring medium and low viscosity (pourable) acrylic paints, water is only necessary if the mixture is too thick, even after adding a little additional pouring medium. Water weakens acrylic paint, so it should be added in the most conservative amount possible. Ideally, this is less than 20 to 30% of the total mixture volume to prevent the paint from developing cracks.

Tip: Use distilled or filtered water, as minerals or contaminants in tap water can affect the paint.

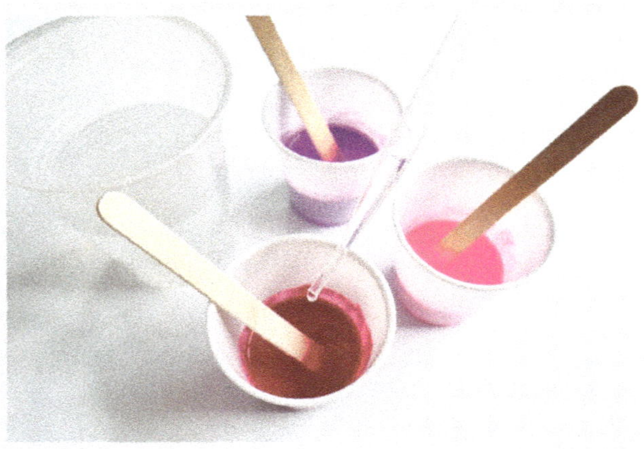

To add water, use a small plastic pipette or dropper or a squeezable plastic bottle (the kind used to water small succulent plants) to control the amount added and prevent over-thinning the paint.

8. AVOIDING AIR BUBBLES IN PAINT

If air bubbles are in the paint mixtures, it's ideal to let them dissipate before starting a painting. Depending on the products used and how much stirring was done, this can take between twenty minutes and twelve hours or more.

If paint cups need to sit longer than an hour, cover them with plastic food wrap and seal them with a rubber band to prevent the paint from thickening. Cups sealed this way should be fine for about twelve hours.

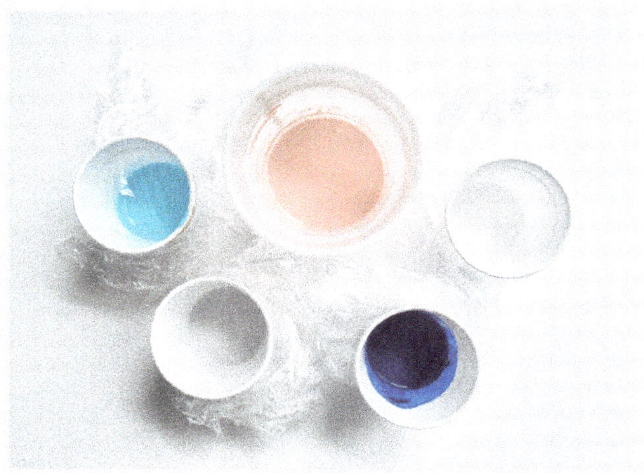

Mixing cups covered with plastic food wrap to keep the paint fresh

If a painting with cells is your goal, air bubbles aren't always bad. They sometimes (but not always) become cells as they pop, so this is something to experiment with.

If there are just a few air bubbles on the canvas after the paint has been poured, they can be carefully popped with a round toothpick or sewing pin.

9. USING PAINT ADDITIVES FOR CELLS (OPTIONAL)

If you plan to use a paint additive, a minimal amount should be added to the paint mixture just before pouring. Here are general guidelines for using additives with acrylic paint.

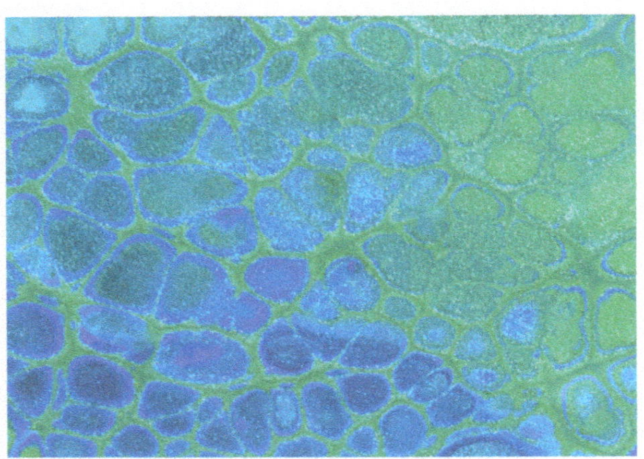

Silicone Oil or Dimethicone-Based Products

Add one drop per 5 to 6 US fluid ounces (148 to 177 mL) of paint mixture. If needed, adjust the number of drops in future paintings.

Once added, use a craft or mixing stick to fold the additive into the mixture. Minimal stirring can make larger cells, while more stirring will create smaller ones. Since this can vary, take time to experiment.

Isopropyl Alcohol (91% or 70%)

Isopropyl alcohol affects acrylic paint in a way that often produces cells and web-like patterns called "lacing." To use it as an additive, try one drop per 5 to 6 US fluid ounces (148 to 177 mL) of paint mixture, and adjust the amount in future paintings if necessary.

Notes for Using Additives

- You'll find that less is more with additives. If too much is added, it can reduce paint adherence or leave sunken areas on the painting surface.
- The amount of an additive needed varies by paint and pouring medium type and combination, so it may take some trial and error to find the best amount to get cells in a painting.
- If the bottle doesn't have a drop-by-drop dispenser, use a plastic pipette or dropper to add a precise amount to your paint mixtures.
- Getting cells in pour paintings can take practice and experimentation to find the right combination of products and techniques. For more tips for increasing the chances of cells, refer to Chapter 24 (Section 9).

10. PREPARING HEAVY BODY ACRYLICS FOR POURING

Although acrylic paints in a fluid form are the easiest to use for pouring, heavy body acrylics (thick paints in tubes) can be used if they're thinned down enough to make them pourable. Here are the steps to do this.

Step 1: Squeeze a small amount of paint into a mixing cup or container.

Step 2: Add a small amount of pouring medium to the paint and slowly stir with a craft stick.

Step 3: Repeat Step 2 until the paint/pouring medium mixture is the same consistency as the pouring medium. Be sure the mixture is smooth, lump-free, and drips down from the craft stick in a steady steam.

This process can leave air bubbles in the paint mixture, so give them time to dissipate before starting a painting.

By thinning heavy body acrylics with pouring medium instead of water, they'll be less likely to crack as they dry. If you want to use water, limit the amount to less than 20 to 30% of the total mixture volume.

11. STORING PRE-MIXED PAINT

To store paint mixtures for extended periods of time, pour them into plastic squeeze bottles or small glass containers with tight sealing lids. This will keep the paints fresh for at least several days and up to a few weeks, depending on the products used.

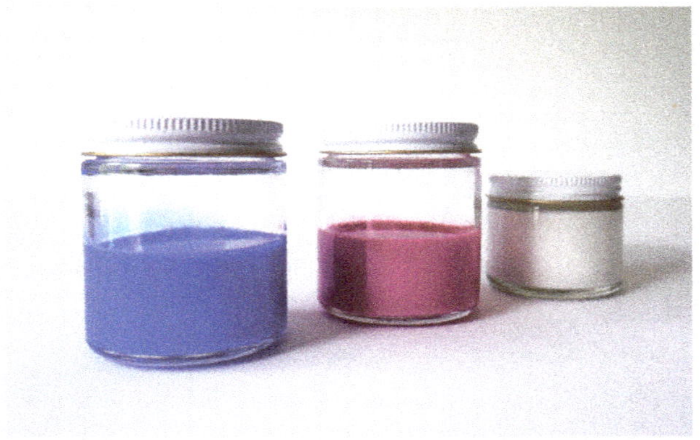

Bottles or containers are also a good option for those who like to pre-mix paints and have them ready to use at any time. If it's been a while since the color was mixed, it might need some re-stirring before use if the products have separated.

Tips:

- If you frequently pre-mix paints and store them in plastic bottles, consider using HDPE (high-density polyethylene) bottles because they're made with materials that won't affect the paint and medium.
- Label the bottle with the paint and medium brand, color, and date mixed.

- Always store paint cups, bottles, or containers at an average room temperature, out of direct sunlight, and out of reach of children and animals.

painting prep & pouring technique instructions

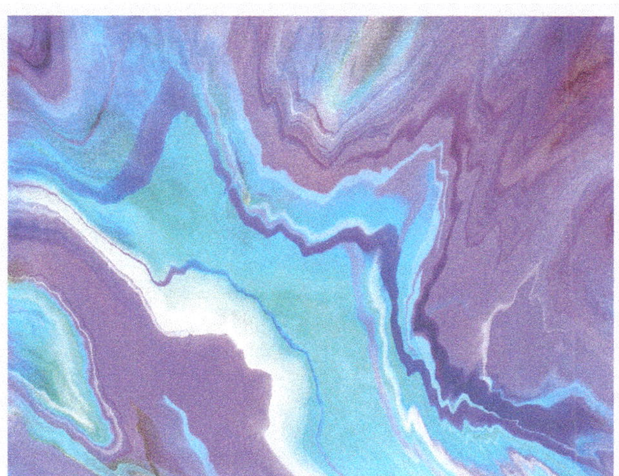

ONCE THE PAINTS ARE MIXED AND YOU'RE READY TO PAINT, THIS CHAPTER explains how to set up a workspace and provides instructions for several popular pour painting techniques. You'll also learn composition and color tips, what optional tools to use to make designs in the paint, how to pour on a flexible painting surface, and how long artwork needs to dry before varnishing.

In this chapter, "canvas" describes any non-flexible painting surface, such as stretched canvases, wood panels, ceramic tiles, or glass.

1. PRE-PAINTING STEPS AND WORKSPACE SET-UP

Here are a few steps to take before starting a painting.

Protect the Work Area

Use a plastic painting drop cloth or plastic sheeting to cover your table or work surface. A large plastic trash bag can be used as an alternative, although it won't cover as much area. If you're working in a space with wood flooring, rugs, carpeting, or another type of surface that could be difficult to clean, that should also be protected.

Protect Your Clothing

No matter how careful one is, paint or pouring medium sometimes gets on clothing. For this reason, I suggest wearing an apron and clothing you don't care about. Although acrylic paints and pouring medium are water soluble, they can be challenging to remove from fabric, especially after they dry.

Tip: If you get paint or pouring medium on clothing, carpet, a rug, a towel, or other fabric, rinse it right away with plenty of water. A laundry stain removal product or liquid dish soap can also help remove paint stains. Try to remove the stain while it's fresh for the best chances of success.

Gather All Needed Items

Place all items needed to paint in your covered work area. This includes the canvas, paint and pouring medium mixtures, a paint additive (optional), disposable gloves, safety glasses, a few crafts sticks and/or a palette knife, paper towels, toothpicks to pop air bubbles, and any other supplies you plan to use.

Set Up the Raised Surface

The canvas must be placed on a raised surface to let the paint flow over the sides. Several options for this include:

- Four upside down plastic beverage cups
- Four empty metal food cans, soup size or smaller
- Wire cooling rack
- Four plastic furniture risers (for large or heavy painting surfaces)

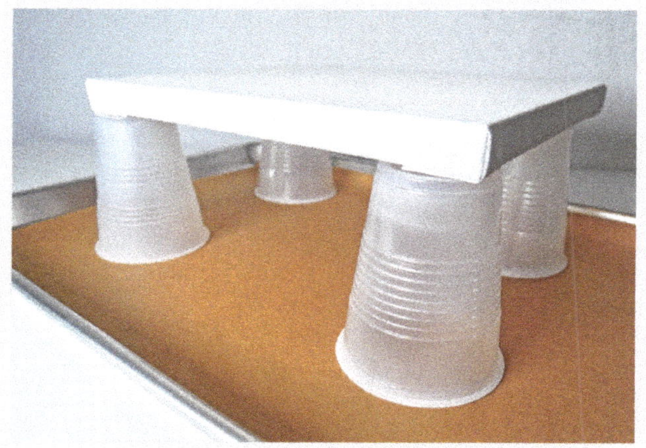

A canvas raised on plastic beverage cups

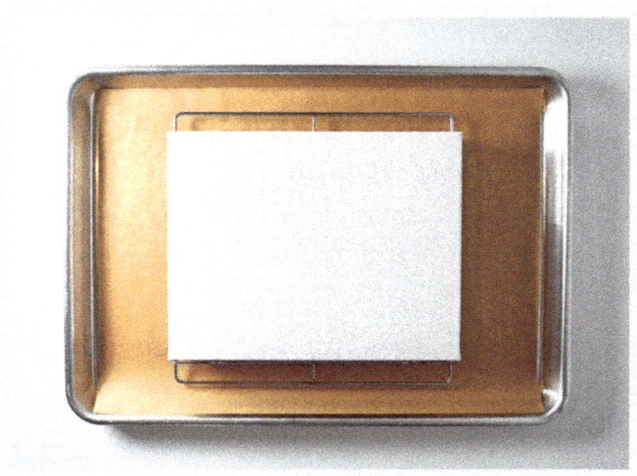

A canvas raised on a wire cooling rack

Contain the Paint for Easier Clean-Up

Post-painting clean-up is easier if the paint is contained. One option is to place a disposable aluminum baking or cookie pan beneath the raised painting. Although this won't work for large canvases, it's ideal for those 10 x 10 inches (25 x 25 cm) or smaller.

Tip: Line the pan with wax or parchment paper; it should stay clean enough to use again. Secure the paper by adding tape to each corner.

Disposable aluminum pan lined with parchment paper

If you don't have a pan, I suggest lining the area beneath the raised canvas with parchment paper or a large silicone craft mat. This will allow for easier clean-up and should keep your drop cloth or sheeting clean enough for future painting sessions.

Tip: Let the colorful puddles of paint runoff dry and save them for other creative art projects. See Chapter 17 to learn more about acrylic skins.

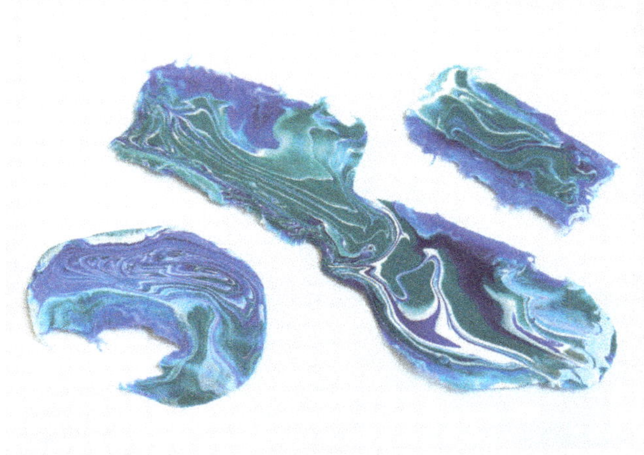

Acrylic skins

Use a Level

If you have a level, place it on the canvas to be sure it's even. Pouring on a level surface will prevent paint from pooling unevenly on the painting.

Tip: If you don't have a level, a smartphone level app also works.

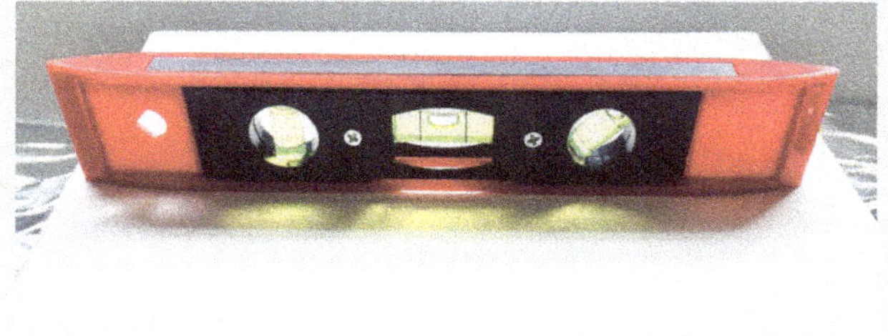

Torpedo level

2. POURING TECHNIQUE INSTRUCTIONS

Artists can use many pour painting techniques to give their paintings a specific style, design, or pattern type. The ones included here are some of the most commonly used, starting with the easiest and concluding with one that's slightly more advanced. It's possible to use several techniques in a painting, but I suggest using just one until you've mastered it.

You'll discover that many factors can influence how a painting turns out, even when using the same technique. A few of these include the number of colors used, the type or brand of paints and pouring medium, and whether a paint additive is put into the mixtures. A minor change or two can produce a painting with a completely unique look.

Although there are infinite ways to pour paint, there aren't any absolute rules. Try new ideas, make modifications, or put your own spin on any aspect of the process. This is your opportunity to get creative and make your painting into anything you want.

TRADITIONAL POUR

The traditional pour is a simple technique that I suggest new painters try for their first few paintings. It's done by pouring paint colors directly from cups onto the canvas. This can be done randomly or in any way you like.

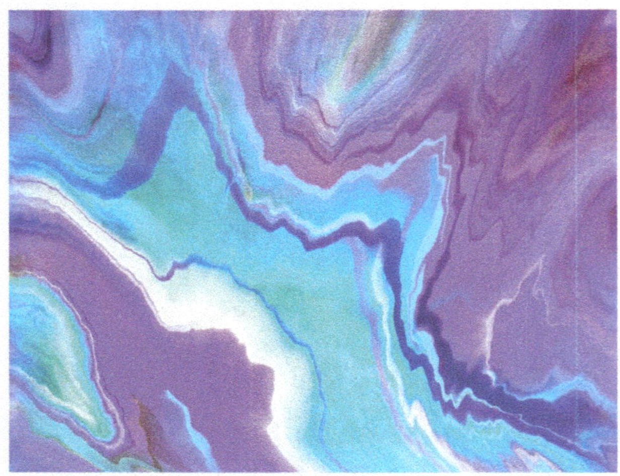

A traditional pour with violet, lavender, aqua, white, iridescent gold, and light blue

Traditional Pour Instructions

Step 1: Mix the paint, pouring medium, and optional additive as described in Chapter 15, using individual paint cups for each color.

Use at least three or four colors.

Step 2: Place the canvas on a level, raised surface and pour colors from each cup in any order or fashion. A few ideas include circles, spirals, lines, swirls, a figure-eight pattern, or a random design of your choice.

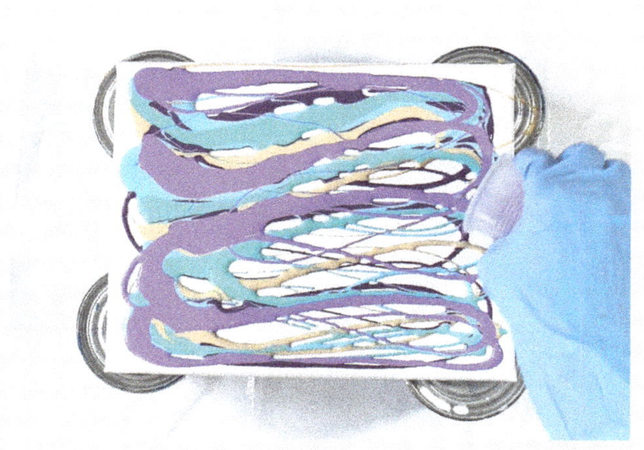

Pouring colors in large swirls

Be sure to pour some paint onto each of the four corners of the canvas.

Try to leave some extra paint in a few of the cups in case it's needed later on.

Step 3: Carefully lift the canvas from its raised surface and slowly tilt it in various directions to let the paint move and flow. It's fine for some paint to spill over the sides but avoid losing too much until the canvas is fully covered.

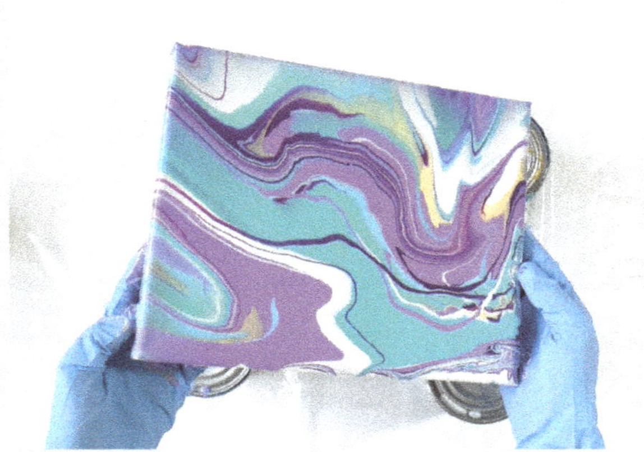

Slowly tilting the canvas to blend the colors

Try to pour off enough paint so there's not an overly thick layer of paint on the canvas without losing the best parts of your design.

If necessary, add leftover paint from the cups and move the canvas to blend it in.

Continue tilting the canvas until the surface is fully covered with paint and you're happy with the painting's overall composition, patterns, colors, and appearance.

Step 4: Return the canvas to its raised surface.

Step 5: If the sides of the canvas aren't completely covered with paint, use a craft stick or palette knife to take some wet paint from beneath the canvas and cover the bare sections.

Step 6: Allow the painting to dry for at least two to four days before moving it.

Step 7: Give the painting another three to four weeks to cure, then apply varnish as described in Chapter 21. (Optional)

DIRTY FLIP CUP POUR

The always fascinating flip cup pour starts with a "dirty pour" cup, which is a cup filled with multiple paint colors. Instead of pouring paint directly from the cup, it's "flipped" onto the canvas and produces a puddle of paint with radiant designs and unexpected colors.

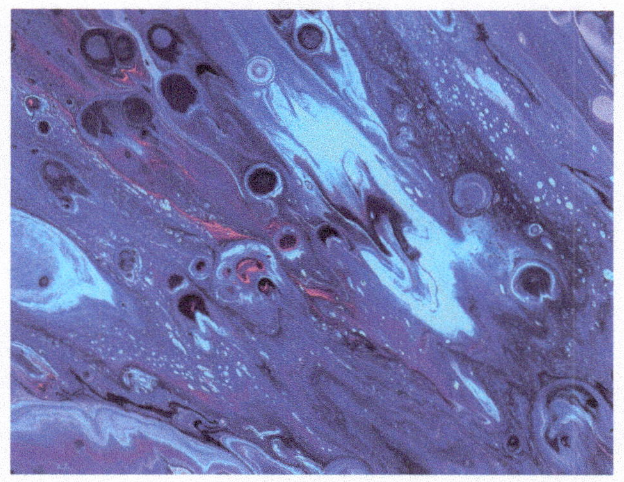

A dirty flip cup pour painting with cells

Dirty Flip Cup Pour Instructions

Step 1: To create a dirty pour cup, mix the paint, pouring medium, and optional additive as described in Chapter 15, using individual paint cups for each color.

Use at least three or four colors.

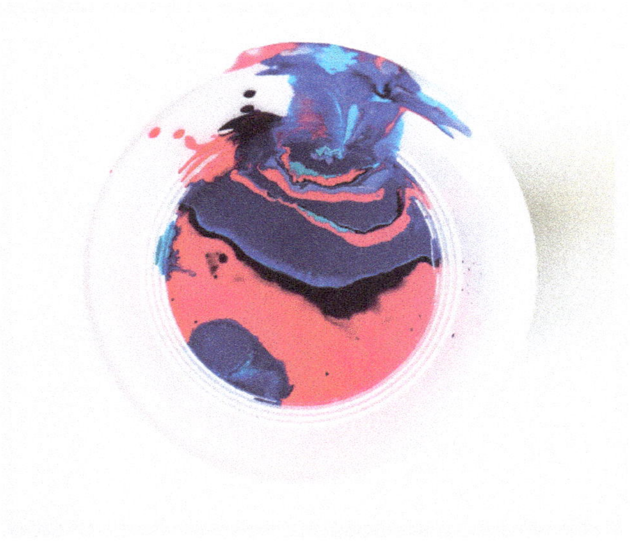

Dirty pour cup

Step 2: Pour each paint color from the individual cups into one larger cup that's approximately 9 to 16 US fluid ounces (266 to 473 mL).

Colors can be poured in layers, one at a time, or by adding small amounts of each color until all the individual cups have been emptied into the larger cup.

Tips:

- Ensure the cup isn't too full or "flipping" it will be more difficult.
- If a painting with cells is your goal, pour the densest color into the cup first. A color like titanium white is a good choice for this.
- For better color separation, pour the individual colors slowly down the sides of the dirty pour cup rather than dumping them into the center.

Optional: After all the colors are in the larger cup, a craft or mixing stick can be used for a very light, quick stir. Keep this to a bare minimum to prevent muddy colors.

Step 3: Place the canvas face down on the dirty pour cup.

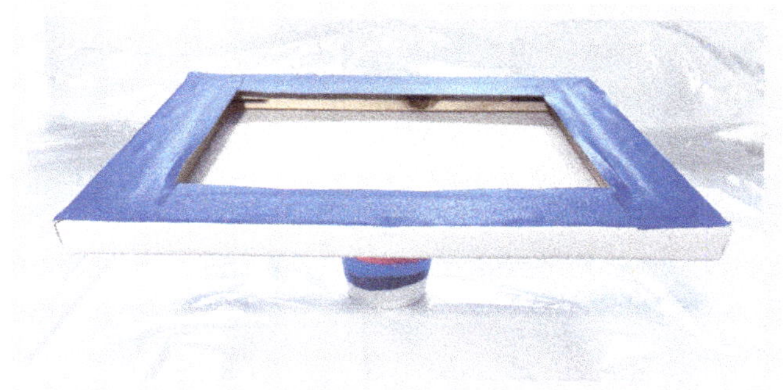

Canvas face down on a dirty pour cup

Step 4: Hold the canvas and cup tightly together so that no paint can spill out, and then "flip" them so the cup is upside down on the canvas.

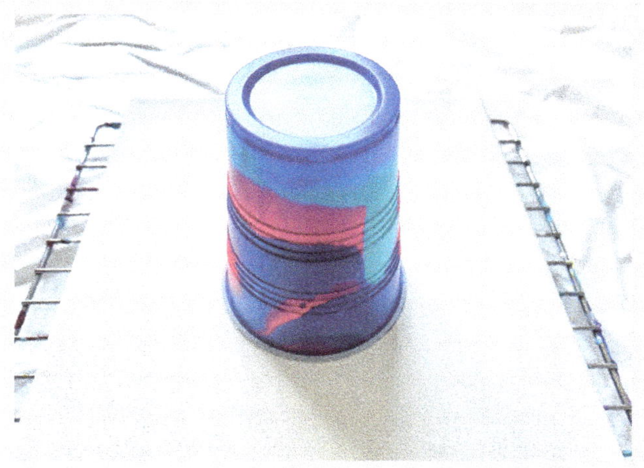

Dirty pour cup sitting on the canvas

Place the canvas and cup on a level, raised surface and wait for thirty to forty seconds for the paint to drip down to the bottom of the cup.

Step 5: Lift the cup to let the paint spill out in a puddle across the canvas.

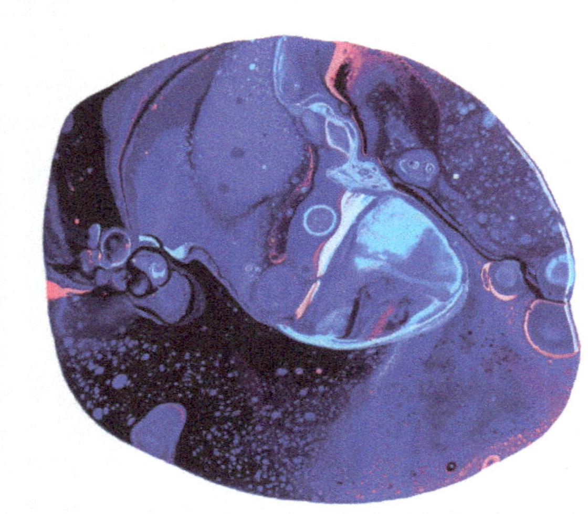

Paint puddle

Step 6: Carefully lift the canvas from its raised surface and tilt it slowly in various directions to let the paint move and flow. It's fine for some paint to spill over the sides but avoid losing too much until the canvas is fully covered.

Try to pour off enough paint, so there's not an overly thick layer of paint on the canvas without losing the best parts of your design.

Continue tilting the canvas until the surface is fully covered with paint and you're happy with the painting's overall composition, patterns, colors, and appearance.

Step 7: Return the canvas to its raised surface.

Step 8: If the sides of the canvas aren't completely covered with paint, use a craft stick or palette knife to take some wet paint from beneath the canvas and cover the bare sections.

Step 9: Allow the painting to dry for at least two to four days before moving it.

Step 10: Give the painting another three to four weeks to cure, then apply varnish as described in Chapter 21. (Optional)

Dirty Flip Cup Notes:

Once you've mastered a dirty flip cup pour, try a "Double Flip Cup" with two dirty pour cups.

NEGATIVE SPACE POUR

Negative space pours feature a solid color around all or part of the primary design or "subject." This bold and creative technique lets artists use their favorite pouring method for the subject and color of choice as the negative space.

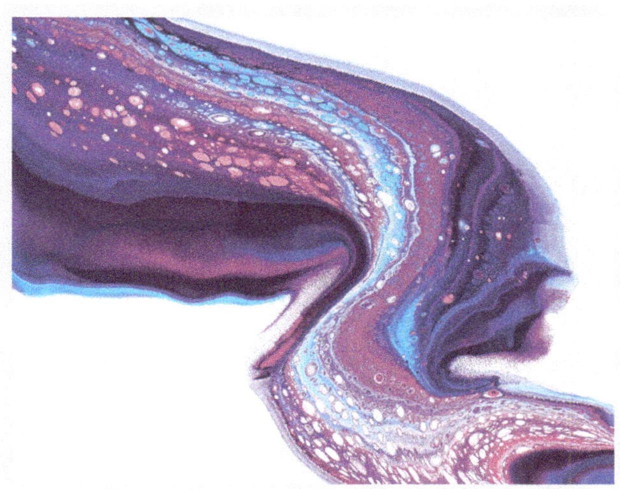

Negative space pour painting

You'll need at least two or three colors for the main design and an additional color for the background. Or, try a two-color negative space pour with black and white.

Negative Space Pour Instructions

Step 1: Mix the paint, pouring medium, and optional additive as described in Chapter 15, using individual paint cups for each color.

Prepare a larger amount of the "negative space" color. This can be white, black, or any other color. Slightly less paint is needed for the subject because it usually takes up less space on the canvas.

Step 2: Place the canvas on a level, raised surface and pour the negative space (background) color onto the canvas. Use a sufficient amount of paint to cover the surface. Fill in any bare sections by moving paint with a clean craft stick, palette knife, or by tilting the canvas until it's thoroughly and evenly covered.

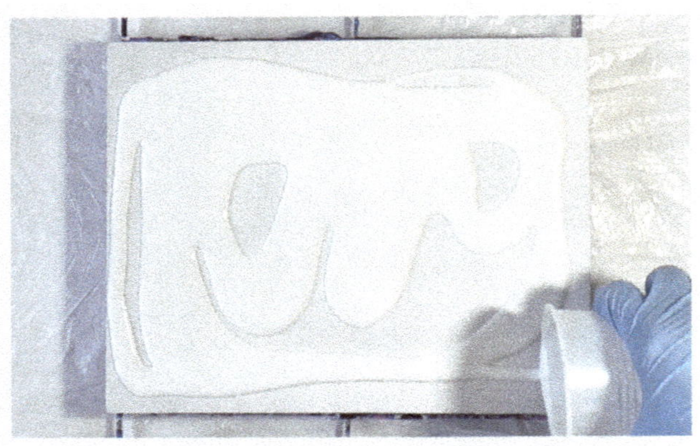

Pouring white as the negative space color

Step 3: Pour the "subject" colors using any pouring method you like. A few simple ones to try are the traditional pour, puddle pour, or pour paint from a dirty pour cup, as I did in the next photo.

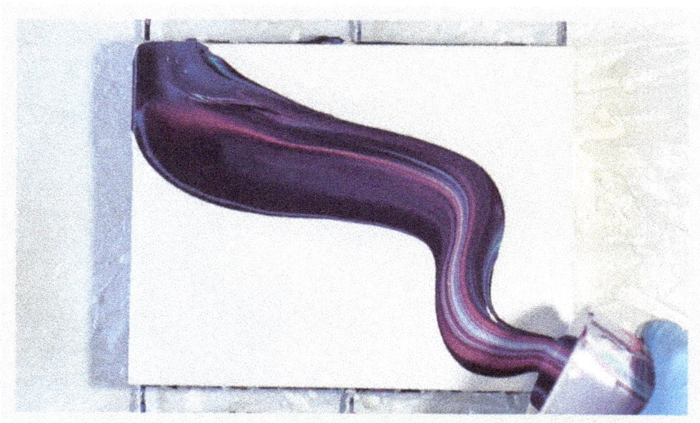

Pouring the primary design from a dirty pour cup

Step 4: Pick up the canvas and slowly tilt it to move the paint around. The goal is to blend the subject colors and let them flow into a design you like while maintaining a negative space around all or part of the subject.

Step 5: When finished, return the canvas to its raised surface.

Step 6: If the sides of the canvas aren't completely covered with paint, use a craft stick or palette knife to take some wet paint from beneath the canvas and cover the bare sections.

Step 7: Allow the painting to dry for at least two to four days before moving it.

Step 8: Give the painting another three to four weeks to cure, then apply varnish as described in Chapter 21. (Optional)

PUDDLE POUR

The puddle pour is a beginner-friendly technique that produces eye-catching abstract designs. This method can be done with just a few colors or many. Like the other techniques, a paint additive is optional. The puddles will have sharper lines without one.

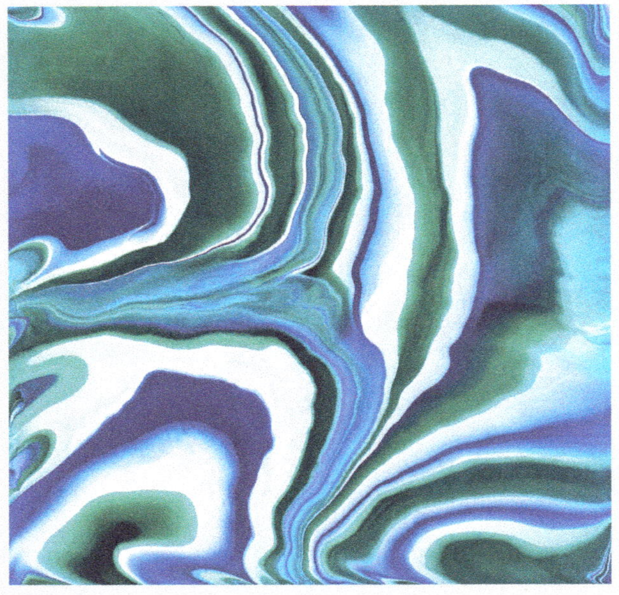

A puddle pour with blue, green, and white

Puddle Pour Instructions

Step 1: Mix the paint, pouring medium, and optional additive as described in Chapter 15, using individual paint cups for each color.

Use at least three or four colors, or try a minimalist color scheme such as black and white.

Tip: Paint can be poured directly from cups or plastic squeeze bottles. You may find that bottles give better control over the amount and placement of the paint on the canvas.

Step 2: Place the canvas on a level, raised surface and pour a small amount of one color from a paint cup onto the canvas in a round "puddle" formation.

Step 3: Pour a small amount of another color in the center of the first, like a bullseye.

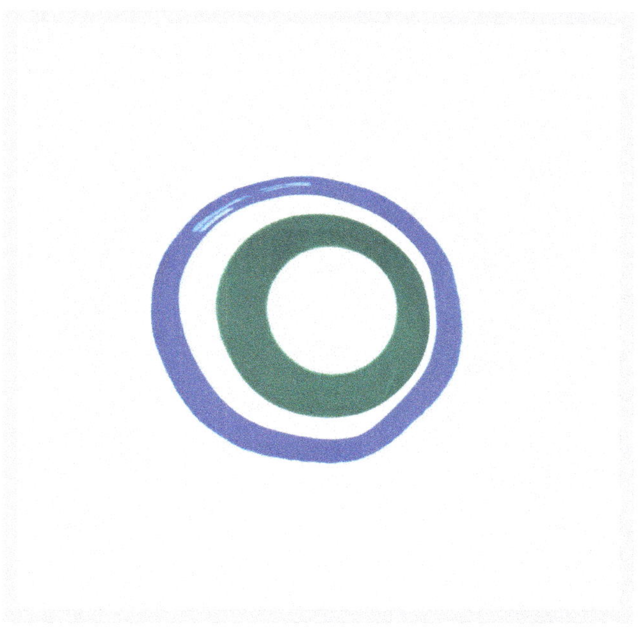

Starting a single paint puddle

Step 4: Continue to pour colors in this manner, in layers on top of each other, until it looks like enough paint has been poured to cover the canvas.

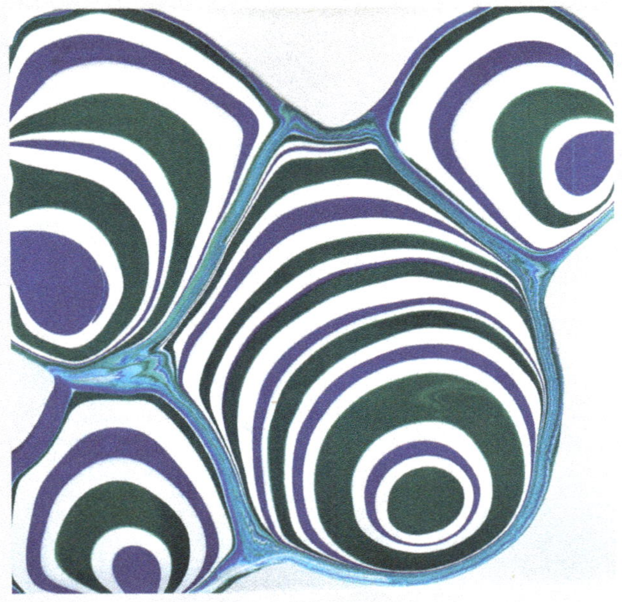

An example of multiple paint puddles

Tips:

- There can be a single paint puddle, two, or many. It's up to you.
- If you want the puddles to maintain their shapes, use enough paint so that extensive tilting isn't necessary.

Step 5: Carefully lift the canvas from its raised surface and tilt it slowly in various directions to let the paint move and flow. It's fine for some paint to spill over the sides but avoid losing too much until the canvas is fully covered.

Moving the canvas in a circular motion can help the puddles keep their round shapes.

More tilting will cause the puddles to spread out and have a ribbon-like appearance, which is also a unique look.

Continue tilting the canvas until the surface is fully covered with paint and you're happy with the painting's overall composition, patterns, colors, and appearance.

Step 6: Return the canvas to its raised surface.

Step 7: If the sides of the canvas aren't completely covered with paint, use a craft stick or palette knife to take some wet paint from beneath the canvas and cover the bare sections.

Step 8: Allow the painting to dry for at least two to four days before moving it.

Step 9: Give the painting another three to four weeks to cure, then apply varnish as described in Chapter 21. (Optional)

BEACH POUR

The beach pour is one of my favorites. The one I describe here utilizes the traditional pour technique, but instead of pouring colors randomly, they're placed to create the appearance of waves and sand.

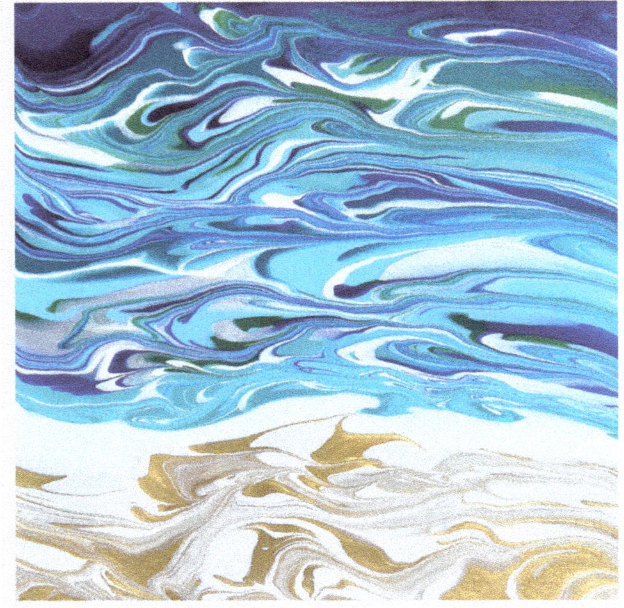

Beach pour

Since this pour is more advanced, I suggest trying it after you've done a few paintings with the traditional pour.

This beach pour requires about seven different colors. Less paint is needed for the sand colors because they'll only be used in the lower quarter or third of the canvas. Here are the shades I suggest using.

Note: Paint color names vary by brand.

Colors for Water

1. Dark Blue, Phthalo Blue, or Navy
2. Emerald Green

3. Turquoise or Aqua
4. Light Blue (or mix blue and white)
5. White or Iridescent White

Colors for Sand

1. Medium or Dark Gold (regular or metallic)
2. Light Beige (or mix gold with white)

Color for Divider Line/Waves

1. White or Iridescent White

Beach Pour Instructions

Step 1: Mix the paint, pouring medium, and optional additive as described in Chapter 15, using individual paint cups for each color.

Step 2: Place the canvas on a level, raised surface and pour a wavy 3/4 to 1-inch thick (1.9 to 2.5 cm) "divider" line of white paint about two-thirds of the way down the canvas. This will help keep the water and sand colors separate.

A wavy divider line of white paint

Step 3: Pour the water shades onto the portion of the canvas above the white divider line. This can be done in any way; however, pouring wavy horizontal lines and swirls will best create the appearance of flowing ocean waves.

Typically, the darkest shades should be poured near the top portion of the canvas, the medium shades in the middle, and the lightest near the bottom, close to but not touching the divider line.

Thin streaks of lighter colors can be poured onto the upper and middle sections to create dimension and add contrast.

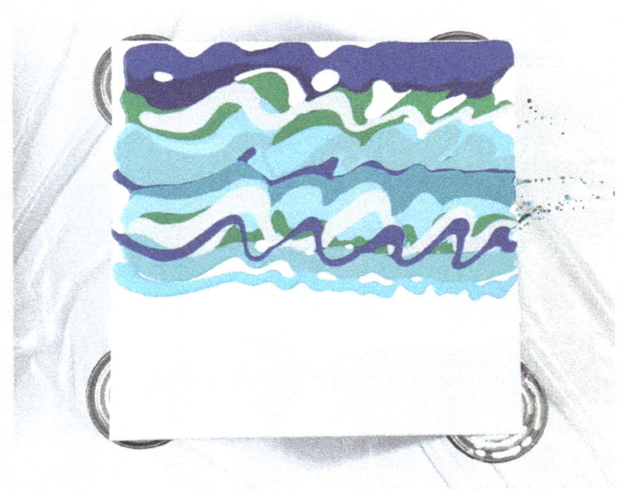

The water colors poured above the white divider line

Leave a small amount of paint in a few of the cups in case you need to fill in any empty spaces later on.

Step 4: Add a few light swirls of white paint over the blue waves to create the look of moving water.

Step 5: Pour the light beige and gold paints onto the lower portion of the canvas to create the look of beach sand. As with the blues, try not to get too close to the divider line.

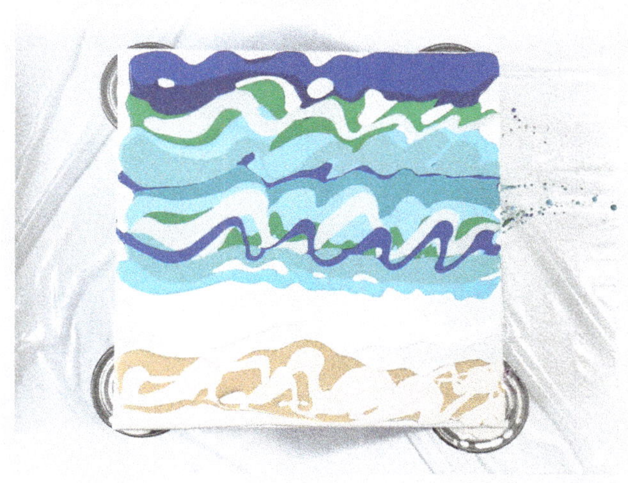

The water and sand colors on the canvas

Optional: Use a clean craft stick to spread paint into empty spaces on the water or sand portions or create wave-like swirls with the wet paint.

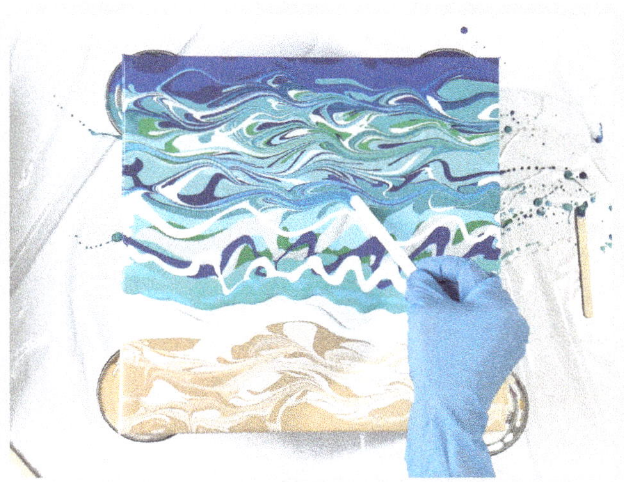

Light blending of colors with a clean craft stick

Step 6: Pick up the canvas and slowly tilt it back and forth **horizontally** to let the colors blend. The goal is to keep the water and sand colors separate, so avoid vertical movements.

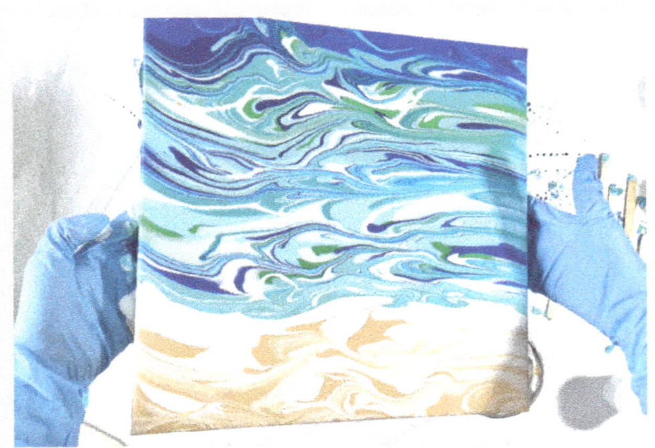

Tilting the canvas horizontally to blend the colors

Continue moving the canvas until paint has covered the entire surface and you're happy with the overall look of the painting.

Step 7: Return the canvas to its raised surface.

Step 8: If the sides of the canvas aren't completely covered with paint, use a craft stick or palette knife to take some wet paint from beneath the canvas and cover the bare sections.

Step 9: Allow the painting to dry for at least two to four days.

Step 10: Give the painting another three to four weeks to cure, then apply varnish as described in Chapter 21. (Optional)

Tips and Ideas for a Beach Pour

Paint Consistency: Be sure the paint mixture is at an optimal consistency. If it's too thin, keeping the water and sand colors separate will be more difficult.

Pour from a Dirty Pour Cup: Put all the colors for the water into a dirty pour cup and pour from this cup instead of individual color cups.

Here are some suggestions if you like metallic paint colors.

- Mix a little iridescent white or silver paint with the colors used in the ocean/waves portion of the painting.
- Add a few thin swirls and streaks of iridescent silver across the water colors.

3. PAINTING COMPOSITION AND COLOR TIPS

Regardless of the pouring technique used, one of the most essential aspects of creating your painting is how you make the paint move and flow. Some pour painters take a minimalist approach and let gravity distribute the paint, so the painting virtually completes itself. Others are more intentional in how they tilt the canvas or use painting tools to move the colors. It's also possible to use a combination of these methods. With pouring, anything goes, and there's no right or wrong way to create.

Here are several things to consider while moving the paint, and before the artwork is complete.

- **Composition:** Do you like the overall design and appearance of the painting on the canvas?
- **Patterns and Designs:** Do you like the look and position of the patterns or designs?
- **Color Balance and Harmony:** Are the colors balanced and aesthetically pleasing?

If there's an area with designs or colors you don't like, it can usually be fixed while the paint is still wet. Here are a few ways to do this.

- Tilt the canvas to let the unwanted colors or designs flow over the sides.
- Continue to tilt the canvas and move the paint around until the overall look of the painting improves.
- Use a palette knife, craft stick, paper towel, or wax paper to scrape off the area that needs improvement. Add some

additional paint and tilt the canvas to blend it with the previously poured paint.

Tip: Having extra paint prepared makes it possible to make corrections or add more colors if needed.

4. TOOLS TO BLEND OR MOVE ACRYLIC PAINT

Tilting the canvas is just one of many ways to blend colors. Here are a few items that can be used to create swirls or other designs or patterns.

- Palette knives
- Craft or mixing sticks
- Drinking straws or coffee stirrers
- Plastic forks
- Toothpicks
- String
- Beaded pull chains for drapery
- Wide-tooth hair combs
- Paintbrushes
- Spackle knives
- Hair dryer or mini air blower

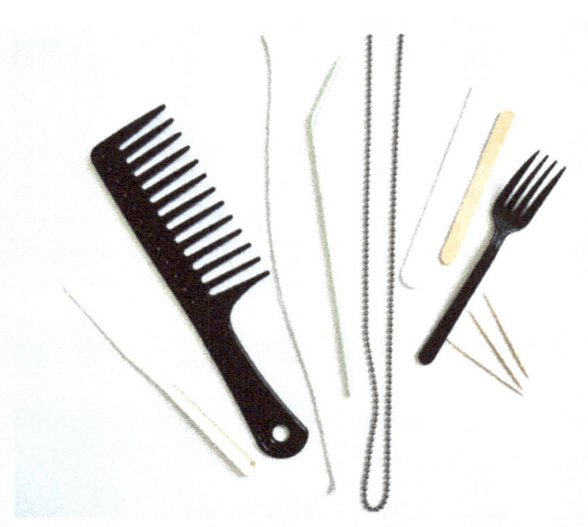

Tips for Using Painting Tools

- Try to finish any work on the painting's surface within the first ten minutes after the initial pour to avoid disturbing the paint once it starts to form a film.
- If using a hair dryer, be sure it's new and clean, or it could leave dust on the painting's surface.
- Take time to practice using these tools with small test paintings before using them on larger pieces.

5. TIPS FOR POURING ON FLEXIBLE PAINTING SURFACES

Flexible painting surfaces such as Yupo® paper, mixed media paper, watercolor paper, or sheets from a canvas pad should be placed directly onto a non-stick surface like plastic sheeting, a silicone craft mat, or parchment paper. This also applies to canvas panels or other surfaces that could warp beneath a layer of wet paint.

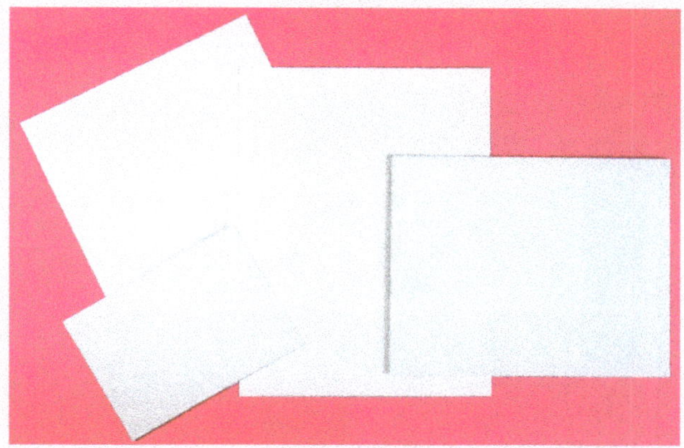

Optional: It's easier to pick up and tilt artwork done on paper or canvas pad sheets if it's placed on a firm backing, like a sheet of corrugated cardboard.

After tilting the painting, carefully slide it from the cardboard onto a clean section of the non-stick surface so it's not sitting in a puddle of paint as it dries.

6. POUR PAINTING DRYING TIMES AND WHEN TO VARNISH

Pour paintings take approximately two to four days to dry. It sometimes takes longer if the layer of paint is thick or in humid conditions. The specific paints and medium used can also affect the drying time.

Avoid touching or moving the painting until you're sure it's dry. To test if it's dry, touch an inconspicuous area on the side to avoid leaving a fingerprint on the surface.

Once dry, the painting can be removed from the raised surface. Since it can take a few weeks for the paint to be dry enough to varnish, store the work on a rack or shelf away from direct sunlight.

To prevent the painting from sticking to a surface, place it on a piece of wax or parchment paper, aluminum foil, a wire cooling rack, or other non-stick material.

If you paint frequently and don't have a place to keep your artwork, consider buying a multi-shelf wire shoe rack to store your works until they're ready to varnish and display.

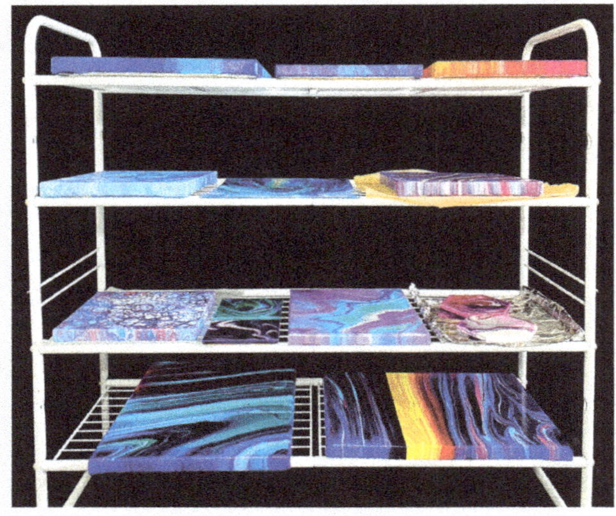

Don't stack acrylic paintings on top of each other because they might stick together and become damaged when they're separated.

If you'd like to varnish a painting, Chapter 21 summarizes varnishing options and offers tips.

more creative pour painting ideas

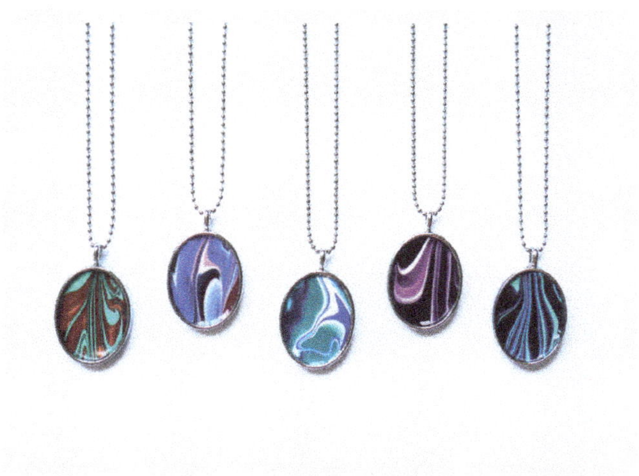

It's impossible to run out of new ideas to try with pour painting. After you've learned a few techniques, explore these other possibilities.

BASE COAT THE PAINTING SURFACE

Adding a base coat to the entire canvas/painting surface will help the colors move more freely. To try this, mix enough paint and pouring medium to cover the surface. For most techniques, the paint mixture should be the consistency described in Chapter 15 (Section 3). White paint is often used as a base coat because it lets other colors stand out, although any color is fine if it's compatible with the colors poured over it.

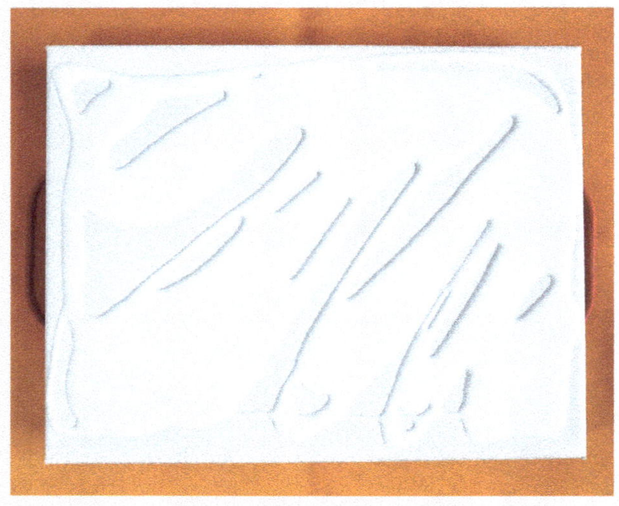

A white base coat poured onto a canvas

After pouring the base coat, tilt the canvas or use a palette knife to distribute the paint and produce a smooth, fully covered surface.

A fully covered surface

Next, use any pouring technique to pour your colors over the wet base coat and continue your painting.

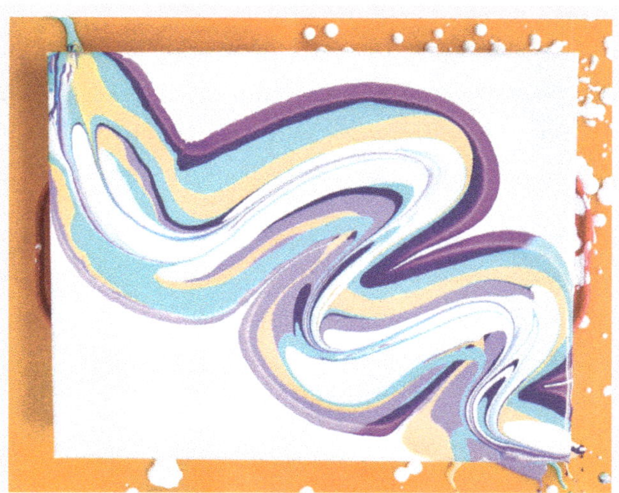

Colors poured over a base coat

POUR PAINT FROM PLASTIC SQUEEZE BOTTLES

Pouring paint from bottles gives better control over where the colors land on the painting surface. It also makes it simple to draw thin lines, circles, fancy swirls, and other fun designs that flow into unique patterns when the paint moves around.

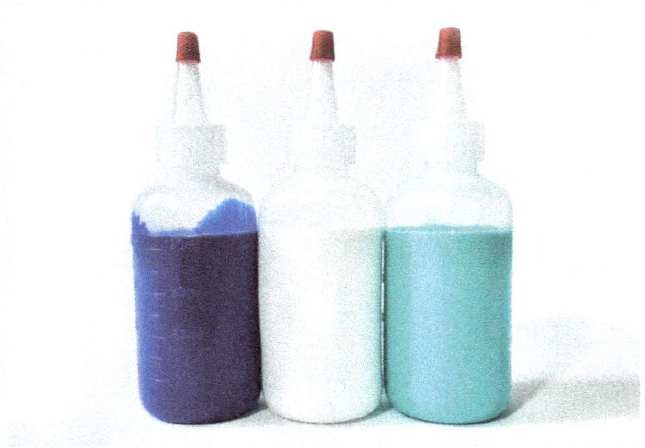

Squeeze bottles are available in assorted sizes at most arts & crafts stores. It is helpful to have small, medium, and large bottles for various sizes of paintings. Avoid bottles with thin metal needle tips because the acrylic paint mixture will be too thick to flow through the openings.

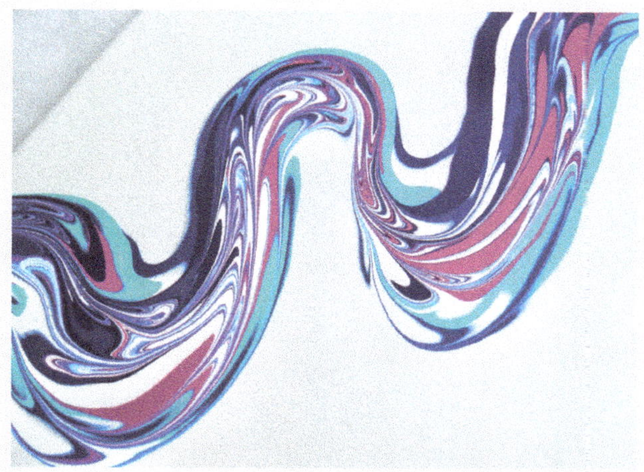

Colorful paints poured with squeeze bottles

Tips for Pouring Paint from Bottles

- Mix the paint and pouring medium in individual cups before pouring it into bottles. A small funnel makes the transfer less messy.
- When using a painting recipe that requires specific amounts of paint and medium, it's a good idea to prepare extra in case some of the mixture is lost in the transfer from cups to bottles.
- Once the bottles are empty, wash them with warm water and liquid dish soap so they can be reused.
- Bottles with leftover paint can be tightly capped and stored for the next painting. Be sure to test the paint before using it to ensure it hasn't become thick or dry. You may need to stir the paint if it's separated.

POUR PAINTING BEVERAGE COASTERS

Colorful beverage coasters are easily made from scratch or with leftover paint from other paintings. Here's what you'll need and a list of steps for this fun project.

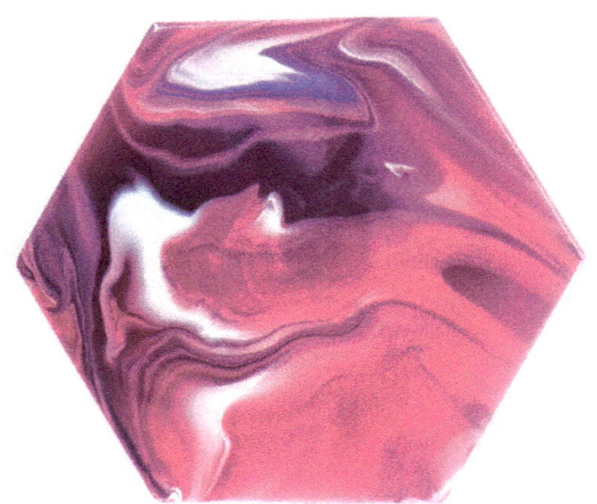

Supplies

- 4 x 4-inch (10 x 10 cm) white or ivory ceramic tiles
- Paint and pouring medium mixtures in at least two to four colors
- Isopropyl alcohol
- Paper towels
- A covering for the table / workspace
- Raised surface (wire cooling rack or food container lids)
- Craft sticks
- Round felt pads with adhesive on back **or** 4 x 4-inch (10 x 10 cm) stick-on cork coaster backings
- Glossy brush-on acrylic polymer varnish
- Varnish brush
- Heat-resistant clear spray
- Optional: Small or medium synthetic bristle artist paintbrush (round or filbert)

Instructions

Step 1: Prepare two to four paint colors in individual cups as described in Chapter 15, or use leftover paint from a previous painting.

Step 2: With some isopropyl alcohol on a paper towel, clean the tile to remove dirt, dust, and fingerprints. Once clean, either handle the tile by the edges or while wearing disposable gloves.

Tip: If you're using an unglazed ceramic tile, see the surface prep steps in Chapter 12 (p. 58).

Step 3: Cover your table or work area with plastic sheeting, a large trash bag, or a silicone craft mat, and place the tile on a raised surface such as a food container lid or wire cooling rack.

Step 4: Pour the paint onto the tile randomly or using any pouring method. After there's enough paint on the tile, pick it up and tilt it to distribute the paint or move it using a craft stick or similar tool. Be sure to pour off enough paint to avoid leaving too thick of a paint layer on the surface.

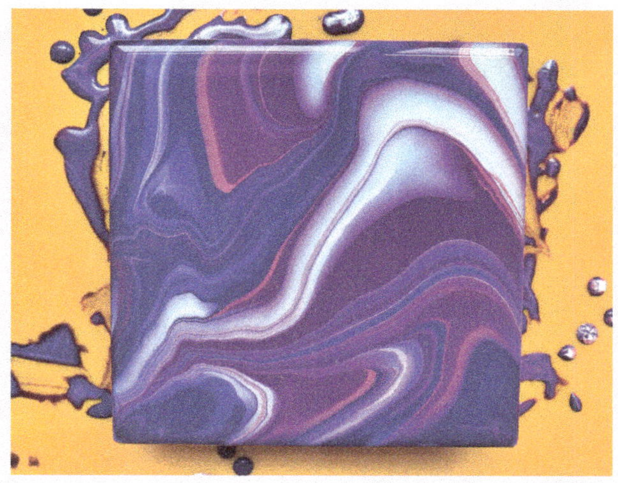

Step 5: Once you like the design and colors, return the tile to the raised surface, and let it dry for one to four days. After that, place it in a clean, dry area out of direct sunlight to cure for about three to four weeks.

Tip: If silicone, dimethicone, or other oil-based additives were used in the paint mixtures, follow the instructions for "Removing Silicone and

Oils from Paintings" provided in Chapter 21 (pp. 142-143) after the paint has had time to cure.

Step 6: (Optional) Use a paintbrush to paint the back of the tile using a color from the painting. Allow it to dry for a few hours, then repeat if necessary.

Step 7: To use the tile as a coaster for hot beverages, apply one or two coats of glossy acrylic polymer varnish to the top, sides, and back. Wait a few days for this to dry, then apply a high-heat enamel spray finish such as Rust-Oleum® High Heat Clear Ceramic Coating (USA) to the coaster's surface. Be sure to follow the safety guidelines on the bottle and the "Spray Varnish Safety Tips" in Chapter 21.

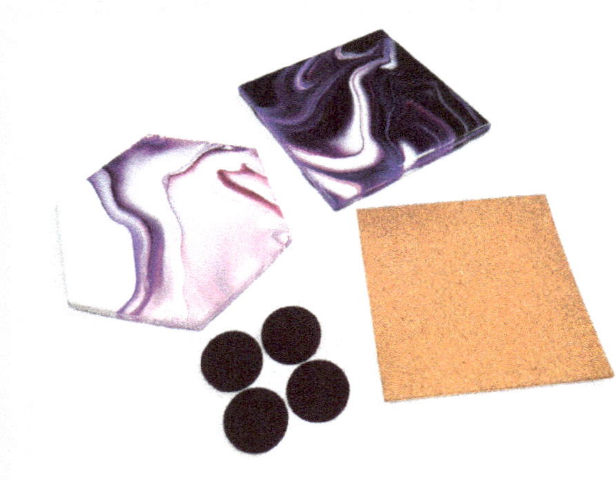

Self-adhesive felt pads and a stick-on cork coaster backing to turn tiles into beverage coasters

Step 8: Give the coating a week to ten days to fully dry, then apply four self-adhesive felt pads or a stick-on cork coaster backing to the back. Now it's ready to use!

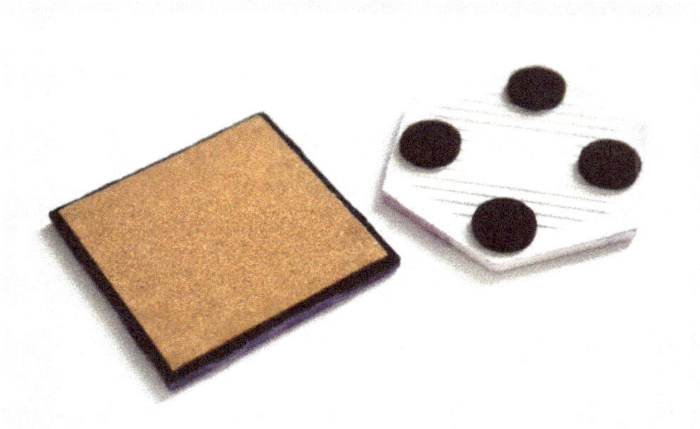

MAKING ACRYLIC SKINS FOR CREATIVE PROJECTS

When dry, acrylic paint becomes a flexible "skin" that can be used for an assortment of creative arts and crafts projects, including mosaics, greeting cards, and jewelry.

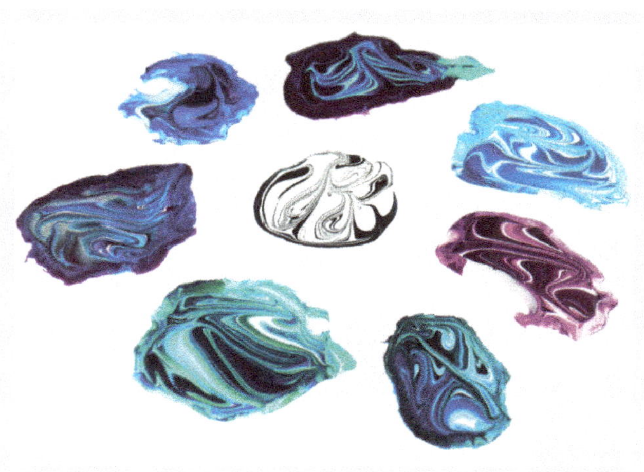

Acrylic skins made for projects

Acrylic skins form on their own from the paint drippings beneath a painting or can be made by pouring paint and pouring medium mixtures directly onto a non-stick surface, such as parchment paper, plastic sheeting, or a silicone craft mat.

Tip: For smooth and ripple-free acrylic skins, use a silicone craft mat. This works best for making jewelry.

Making Acrylic Skins from Pour Painting Runoff

Before starting a painting, place a piece of parchment paper, plastic sheeting (4 mm or thicker), or a silicone craft mat beneath the raised canvas/painting surface. This will catch the paint drippings and make it possible to peel them off when they're dry.

After completing the painting, leave the paint drippings undisturbed on the non-stick surface for at least five to seven days. Drying sometimes takes longer, depending on the room temperature, humidity level, and the thickness of the paint.

When you're sure the paint is dry, carefully peel the skins from the non-stick surface and place them on a sheet of parchment paper, wax paper, or a silicone mat in a flat tray or pan until you're ready to use them. Be sure they don't overlap because they'll likely stick together. Store them at room temperature and out of direct sunlight, but not in a sealed container.

Making Acrylic Skins by Pouring Paint from Cups

Preparing the Paint

To make acrylic skins specifically for art projects or jewelry, mix the paints and pouring medium in individual cups the same way as done for a painting. The paint mixtures should be the consistency described in Chapter 15 (Section 3).

Tip: Acrylic skins can be made with any acrylic paint and pouring medium or gloss medium combination; however, using artist grade paints and mediums will give them a vibrant color intensity and less chance of cracking or fading. This is especially important for creating professional quality projects or for making jewelry.

If air bubbles develop in the paint after stirring, cover the cups with plastic food wrap sealed with a rubber band, or pour the paint into glass or plastic containers that can be tightly sealed. Allow the paint to sit for about twelve hours or until the mixtures appear smooth and bubble-free.

Pouring the Paint

Place your non-stick surface of choice on a flat and completely level surface.

For multi-color acrylic skins, pour puddles or rectangles of paint from a dirty pour cup or use a pouring technique such as the Traditional Pour or Puddle Pour.

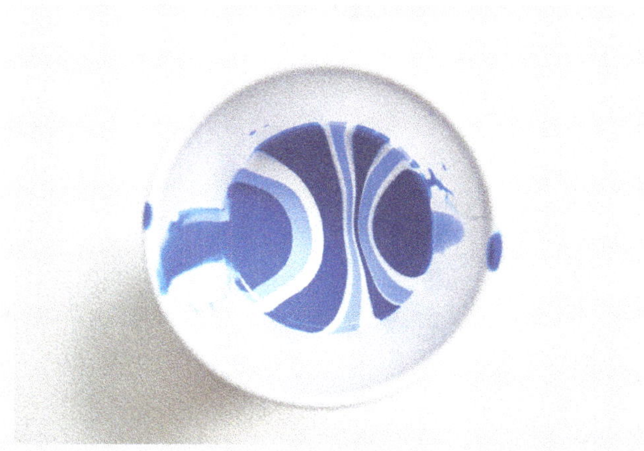

Pouring from a dirty pour cup creates colorful acrylic skins for jewelry and other projects.

To make solid color skins, pour single colors of paint with plenty of space between each to prevent colors from blending.

Paint can be poured into smaller or larger shapes depending on the size and quantity of skins needed for your project.

The paint should be approximately 1/8-inch (3.2 mm) thick for the best results, although it can be slightly thicker or thinner to suit your specific creation.

Optionally, use a craft stick, palette knife, or similar tool to move the paint, spread it out to the proper thickness, or to make swirls or other designs. Avoid over-blending colors, or they'll appear muddy and indistinct.

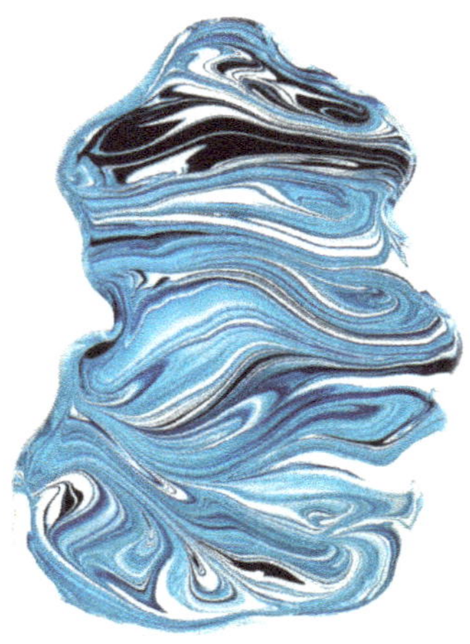

Paint colors swirled with a craft stick

Once finished, allow the paint to dry for a minimum of five to seven days. After you're sure they're dry, carefully peel the skins off and place them on a flat pan or tray between sheets of non-stick parchment paper until you're ready to use them.

Using Acrylic Skins in Projects

Use scissors to cut dried acrylic skins into any size or shape for your project needs. These pieces can be glued to various items, including:

- Ceramic or glass vases
- Blank jewelry bezels to make items such as necklaces, pendants, and earrings
- Card stock to create greeting cards
- A traditional acrylic painting

- The cover of a journal or notebook
- Magnets
- Ornaments

Adhesives that work with acrylic skins include:

- Clear-drying PVA glue
- Acrylic gloss medium
- Acrylic polymer varnish
- Acrylic gel medium
- Jewelry glue (This has strong fumes and should only be used by adults in a well-ventilated location.)

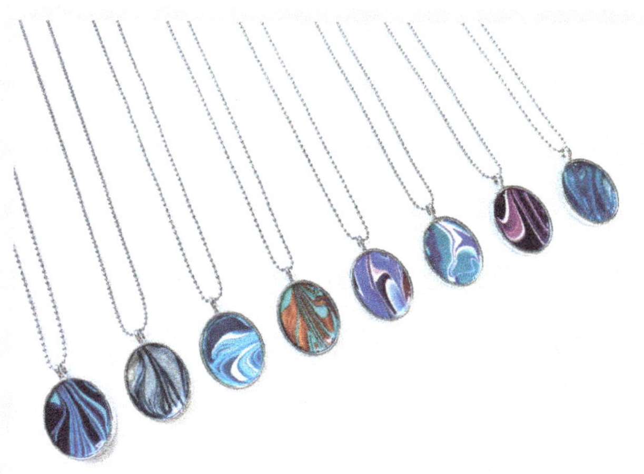

Adding a Protective Topcoat

To protect finished projects and give them a uniform sheen, add two or three coats of an acrylic polymer varnish or acrylic gloss medium after the artwork is dry.

Acrylic resin varnish is another option for protecting jewelry and acrylic skins attached to glass, ceramic, or metal because it has more strength and clarity than other types of varnish. Because of toxic fumes, this type of varnish should be used only by adults in a well-ventilated location. A paint thinner will be needed to clean the brush.

For further information about varnishing, see Chapter 21.

clean-up tips

1. Keep a trash container and some paper towels (or old rags) in the immediate work area to avoid carrying paint-covered items across the floor.

2. Acrylic paint and pouring medium on hands/skin rinses off with soap and water. If the paint has dried, a textured washcloth or bar of pumice grain soap may help remove stubborn stains.

3. Acrylic paint or pouring medium that gets on clothing, towels, carpeting, or other fabrics should be quickly rinsed with water and an appropriate soap or cleanser for the best chances of complete removal. If using a fabric stain removal product, follow the instructions on the bottle for the specific fabric type.

4. Acrylic paints, pouring mediums, gesso, and varnishes shouldn't be poured down sink drains. Not only will they clog drains, but they can enter the water system and potentially cause environmental harm. Instead, pour unwanted products into a container (such as a coffee can) and allow them to dry before disposal. Be sure to store this in a safe place out of reach of children and animals.

Tip: Disposal of artist paint materials varies from place to place, so check with the trash collection company in your area for specifics.

5. To avoid clogging a sink drain, paint, gesso, or mediums on palette knives, paintbrushes, or other painting tools should be thoroughly wiped with a paper towel or paint rag before washing them with a mild liquid dish soap and water.

6. Dried acrylic paint or paint stains on plastic or metal painting tools can usually be removed with some isopropyl alcohol on a paper towel or cotton pad.

7. Leftover paint that you'd like to save for another project can be poured into plastic or glass containers with tight sealing lids. In my experience, paint mixtures can last up to a few weeks when stored like this; however, check to ensure it's still usable before starting a new project.

eco-friendly tips for pour painters

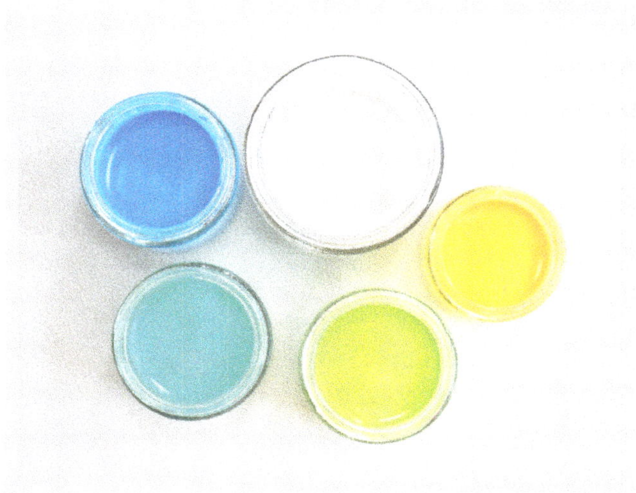

ACRYLIC POURING REQUIRES MORE PAINT AND SUPPLIES THAN OTHER TYPES of acrylic painting. If you're eco-conscious, you may want to know how to minimize the environmental impact of creating with this style of art. This chapter lists a few ways to reduce the amount of leftover paint and supply waste. Adding even one or two of these suggestions to your routine will make a difference, especially for those who paint often.

1. Keep an assortment of extra painting surfaces on hand to make other paintings from leftover paint.

2. Instead of throwing out the puddles of wet paint that pool beneath the painting, let them dry and save them for other arts and crafts projects. See Chapter 17 for details.

Tip: Place a large silicone craft mat or another non-stick surface directly beneath your raised painting. This will make it possible to peel off the dried paint for safe disposal or to use in other projects.

3. Reuse the plastic food wrap and rubber bands used to cover paint mixing cups.

4. Using a whole plastic drop cloth for each painting session is only necessary if you need to cover a large area and flooring. Cut the plastic into smaller pieces and use it for multiple paintings and projects.

5. Reusable glass or silicone containers can serve as an alternative to plastic cups for paint mixing and pouring.

6. Use silicone-coated mixing sticks instead of wood craft sticks. After paint mixing, place the sticks on a non-stick surface to dry. From there, peel off the paint and use the sticks again.

7. Consider upcycling items from secondhand stores for your poured creations. A few ideas include used canvases, glass or ceramic vases or photo frames, wood tables, serving trays, vinyl records, and any other unique glass or wood objects you think would make interesting art.

Be sure to clean, dry, and properly prepare the surface before pouring. Chapter 12 provides information about preparing various surfaces.

8. Unwanted paints, pouring mediums, or other supplies that are still usable can be donated to friends, family, or a local school. Artist groups (in-person or online) are another place to connect with someone who might need supplies.

While these tips are a starting point, I suggest looking for new eco-friendly pouring supplies at your favorite art supply store from time to time or experimenting with ideas you have to make the process greener.

how to touch up a painting's edges

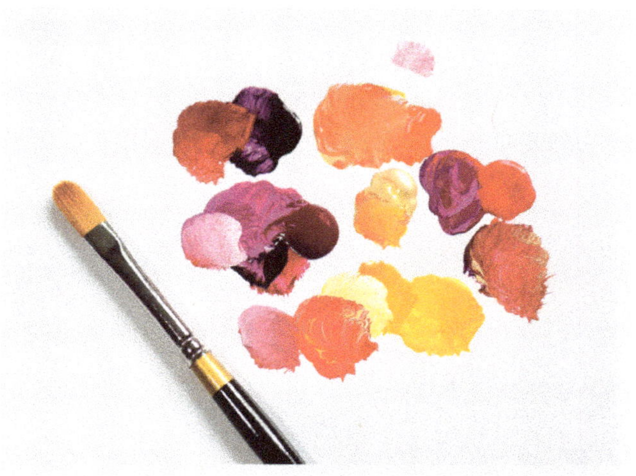

THE EDGES OF A POUR PAINTING CAN BE JUST AS FASCINATING AS THE surface, and you might not want to hide them behind a frame. If they have bare spots, paint smudges, or otherwise look messy, here's how to neaten them up, so they match the rest of the painting.

Supplies

- The paints used for the painting
- Pouring medium or acrylic gloss medium
- Small synthetic bristle artist paintbrush (round or filbert)
- Plastic paint palette or palette paper pad
- A covering for the table/workspace
- Two to four objects to raise the canvas (small empty metal cans, food container lids, or similar)

Instructions

Step 1: Once the painting is completely dry, put small dabs of the same colors used in the painting on a palette or palette paper. If you need to moisten the paint, use a limited amount of pouring medium or an acrylic gloss medium.

Step 2: Use a paintbrush to make neat brushstrokes that mimic the appearance of paint dripping down from the surface. Allow the surface colors to guide color placement on the edges. Be careful not to get paint on your hands and touch the painting's surface while holding the canvas.

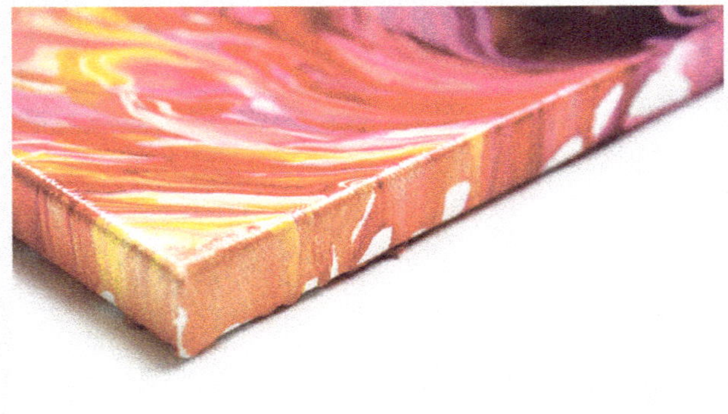

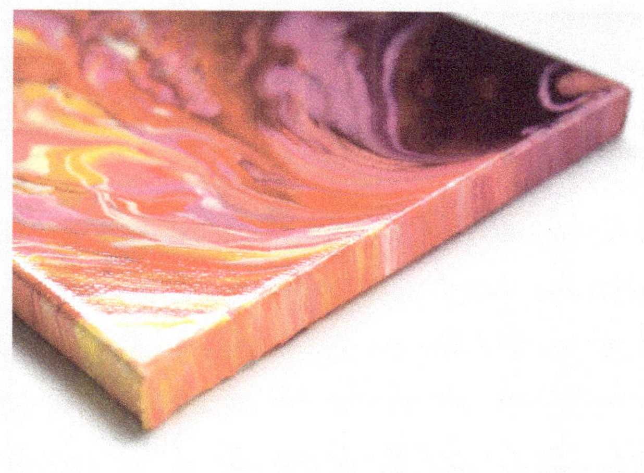

Step 3: Once complete, place the painting on a raised surface and allow the edges to dry.

Tips:

- If the edges need a lot of work, touch up one or two sides at a time. Allow them to dry, then repeat this process with the other sides.
- In the future, practice covering bare spots as you complete the painting, or use a craft stick covered with paint drippings from below the canvas to fill in uncovered sections once the work is on a raised surface.

protecting the finished painting

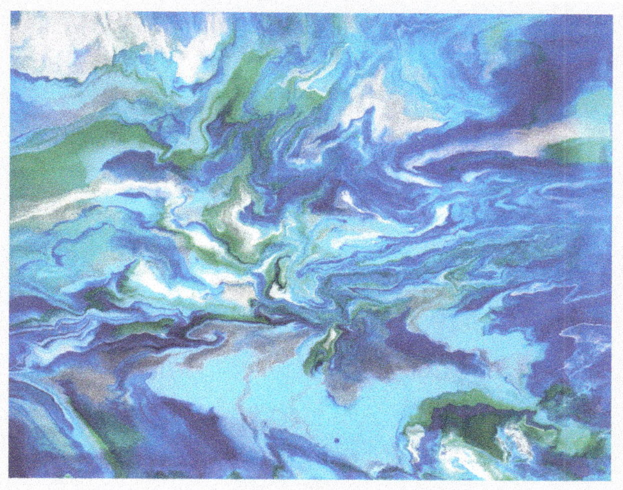

ONCE A PAINTING IS FINISHED AND FULLY DRY, PROTECTING IT WITH varnish can keep it looking fresh and vibrant for years to come. While acrylic pour paintings are more durable than some types of artwork, they can still be damaged by handling, UV light, and various environmental pollutants.

Varnishing a painting is an optional step but one to consider depending on where the art will be kept and if you want it to keep its original color. New painters may not be concerned about the longevity of their earliest works but might want to varnish them to learn the process.

Additional reasons to varnish a painting include unifying an uneven sheen or changing the finish entirely. For example, a lackluster matte finish can be transformed into a resplendent shine simply by adding a coat of varnish.

This chapter explains options to protect acrylic paintings and includes my tips for varnishing success.

WHEN TO VARNISH A PAINTING

Acrylic pour paintings have a thick layer of paint on their surface, so it's best to let them dry for at least three or four weeks before applying varnish. This will give the paint time to cure and prevent potential problems caused by varnishing a painting that's not fully dry. In the meantime, store paintings in a clean and dry location with adequate ventilation.

Tips:

- If you intend to take photos of your artwork, do this before applying varnish. This is especially important if you plan to use a glossy varnish because photographing it can be more challenging. See Chapter 25 for photo-taking tips.
- If you'd like to sign your painting, do this prior to varnishing.

REMOVING SILICONE AND OILS FROM PAINTINGS

Varnish won't properly adhere to art with oil on the surface from silicone oil or other oil-based paint additives. Fortunately, this residue can be removed. I do this by placing the painting in a disposable baking or cookie pan and covering it with a light layer of corn starch.

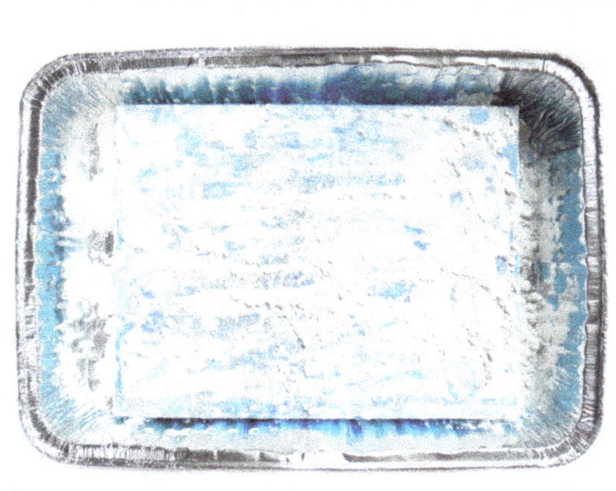

Tip: Large works can be placed directly on a covered table or floor.

Allow the oil to be absorbed for a few hours before brushing off the corn starch and repeating this until the oil is gone. This process is dusty, so I recommend wearing safety glasses and a dust mask.

To ensure all oils are removed, use a soft cloth or sponge with water and mild liquid dish soap to clean the painting surface and sides. Afterward, let the artwork dry for a day or two before applying varnish.

Tip: Always test an edge or small corner of the painting before cleaning the surface with soap and water to be sure it doesn't affect the painting's finish.

AN OVERVIEW OF VARNISH OPTIONS

Pour painters have a variety of varnish types to choose from. Here are a few that are suitable for acrylic paintings.

Acrylic Polymer Varnish (Brush-on)

Acrylic polymer varnish provides a transparent, permanent barrier against physical or environmental damage to acrylic paintings. This type of varnish is water-soluble and doesn't create fumes. It's an excellent choice for beginners and professionals alike because it's archival quality, easy to use, and doesn't require paint thinner for application or brush cleaning.

Acrylic Resin Varnish (Brush-on)

Acrylic resin varnish is solvent-based, removable, and dries to a hard, clear finish. Some resin varnishes need to be thinned with paint thinner for application, and paint thinner is required to clean the brush. Because of its strong fumes, this type of varnish should only be used by adults in a well-ventilated location.

Before applying a resin varnish, adding an "isolation coat" to the painting is recommended, which I explain later in this chapter.

Resin varnishes are best for those with some varnishing experience.

UV-Resistant Varnish Spray

UV-resistant varnish sprays give acrylic paintings a clear, permanent acrylic coating that shields them from the effects of sunlight, handling, and dirt, as well as paint yellowing or discoloration.

UV Archival Varnish Spray

This type of varnish spray offers similar protection to UV-resistant sprays but can be removed if necessary.

SPRAY VARNISH SAFETY TIPS

Because of their toxic fumes, spray varnishes should only be used by adults in a well-ventilated area or outdoors.

Use the spray away from people and animals, and consider wearing a respirator mask to avoid breathing fumes.

If spraying outdoors, don't apply varnish on a windy day.

As with all varnish products, follow the instructions on the bottle for safety, testing, application, and drying times for the best results.

THE IMPORTANCE OF CHOOSING A FINISH

Most varnishes are available in several finishes, including high gloss, glossy, satin, and matte. The choice of a finish affects the overall sheen of the painting and the appearance of the colors. High gloss and glossy varnishes make colors appear more saturated, while satin and matte finish varnishes make them softer and more muted.

ISOLATION COAT

An isolation coat is a permanent, transparent layer applied to the finished painting before adding a final varnish. If the varnish ever needs to be removed because of discoloration or if the artist isn't happy with the application, the isolation coat acts as a buffer to protect the paint from the harsh product used to remove the varnish.

Adding an isolation coat is especially important for painters who plan to apply a satin or matte finish varnish to their paintings. Using these varnishes without an isolation coat sometimes causes colors to appear cloudy.

Tips:

- Wait three or four weeks after finishing a pour painting before applying an isolation coat.
- If you want to sign your painting, do this in advance.
- An isolation coat is a permanent addition to the painting, so apply it as neatly and evenly as a final varnish.
- After application, wait a few days before applying a final varnish or follow the instructions on the bottle.
- Isolation coat products are sold at art supply stores and online.

MY VARNISH RECOMMENDATIONS FOR BEGINNERS

I suggest a brush-on glossy or high gloss acrylic polymer varnish for those new to varnishing. It'll make the colors pop and add a beautiful shine.

If you prefer a spray finish, try a UV-resistant clear acrylic spray.

GENERAL VARNISH APPLICATION TIPS

The following are my tips and suggestions for varnishing paintings.

Practice First

Applying varnish isn't too difficult, but if you haven't done it before, I suggest trying several practice applications before using it on your best paintings. Not only will this help your varnish application be more successful, but you'll get to preview how the finish will look on your art.

There are a few ways to do this. One option is to practice varnishing your least favorite paintings. Another is to use small surfaces, such as 5 x 7-inch (13 x 18 cm) canvas panels to create a few sample paintings with the paint and pouring medium of your choice. Once they're dry, practice varnishing these until you're confident enough to finish your best artwork.

Test Application

I recommend testing any new varnish and isolation coat before using the product or products on the painting. This is the best way to prevent unexpected results.

To do this, create a small test painting using the same paints, medium, and colors on a similar surface as the work you plan to varnish. For example, use a small canvas panel or a half sheet from a canvas pad to test how the varnish will appear on a stretched canvas.

Good Lighting

Work in a well-lit area so you can clearly see where and how the varnish is applied.

Clean the Painting

Just before application, use a clean, dry, soft cloth to wipe any dust, dirt, or fingerprints from the painting. Microfiber cloths (used for cleaning eyeglasses or electronic screens) work well for this step.

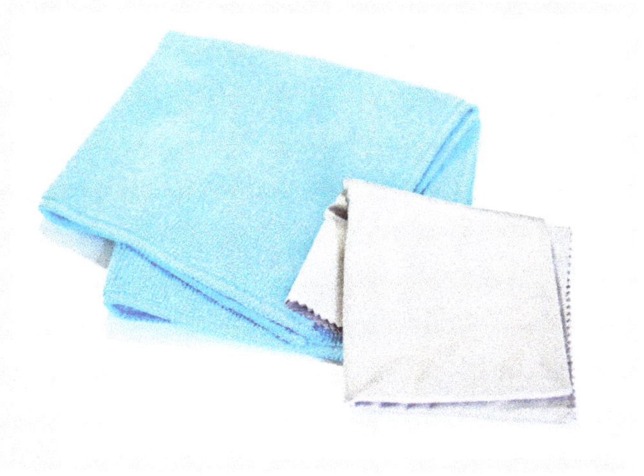

Brush Choice

Use a soft, synthetic bristle brush that doesn't shed bristles. I like mop brushes with rounded edges for varnish application. A wide, flat, color wash brush is another type to consider.

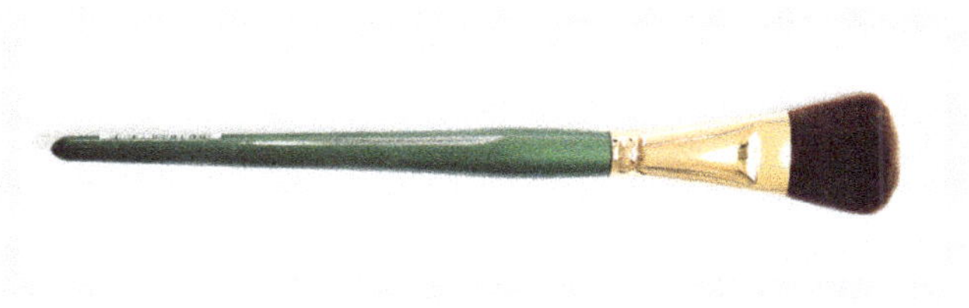

Mop brush for varnishing

Tip: Use your varnish brush for only one type of varnish (water-based or solvent-based) and not for gesso application or general painting. Labeling it with a permanent marker makes it easier to remember.

Number of Coats

Two or three light coats of varnish (allowing for drying time between each) are better than one heavy application. The number of coats required is specific to the type of varnish, so read the bottle for details.

Tip: With any varnish, apply the second coat in the opposite direction as the first to reduce the visibility of brush or spray marks.

Drying Time

After applying the varnish, allow it time to fully dry before touching or moving the painting. Drying times can vary by varnish type and temperature and humidity level in your location, so check the label on the one you use for specific information.

Final Notes on Varnish

Varnish can bring a painting together and enhance its durability so it can be enjoyed for many years. Most varnishing issues that leave an artist with a work they're dissatisfied with can be prevented with practice, testing, and being informed about the products used.

If you ever consider selling your paintings, take time to further explore varnish and isolation coat options, products, and methods to find the best one for your work.

options for displaying or framing a painting

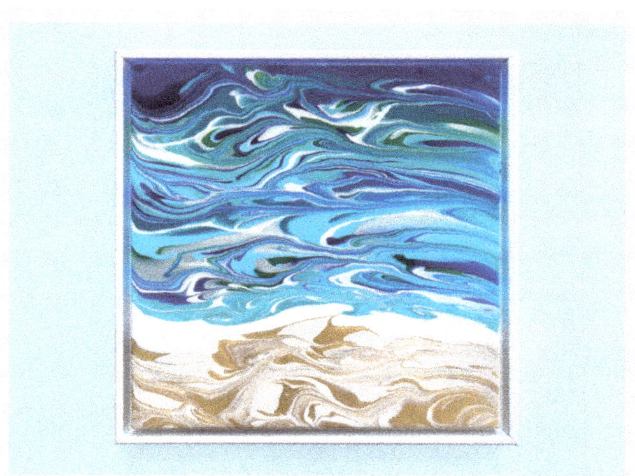

WHEN YOU'RE READY TO SHOW OFF YOUR FINISHED PAINTING, YOU MIGHT wonder what options there are. From modern and minimalist to something more traditional, this chapter provides a quick overview of ways to display your art.

Frameless Display

Hanging a painting without a frame lets the artwork be the star of the show. Staple-free canvases can be displayed without a frame as long as the edges are neat. To hang a painting on a wall, you'll need a picture hanging kit from an art supply or home improvement store.

Framing Artwork

A frame becomes part of a painting, so choosing carefully is essential. The right frame can enhance a piece of art, and the wrong one can detract from it. Since most pour paintings have a myriad of hues and patterns, a simple white, black, or other solid color frame will emphasize the art.

Frame Options

Standard frames are available in wood or metal, and in various colors and styles, from classic to ultra-modern.

Floater frames also work well for pour paintings. This type of frame, as pictured at the beginning of the chapter, resembles a standard frame, except it makes it appear as if the artwork is floating in the center.

Tips for Finding and Choosing a Frame

- Know the exact dimensions of your painting (including the depth) before frame shopping.
- If you prefer unique or vintage frames, browse resale or antique shops or online auction sites for rare finds.
- For guidance on selecting a frame that best showcases your artwork, visit an art supply store that sells frames or a custom framing store.

my tips for new pour painters

As you try more paintings, here are some tips that you may find helpful.

Start Small

Use small canvases or other painting surfaces to reduce supply costs when you're starting out, learning new techniques, or testing new supplies or color ideas.

Extra Paint

Before starting a painting, have extra paint pre-mixed and ready in case you don't have enough paint for the piece you're working on. This is also useful for making corrections or adding more colors.

Pour Painting Supply List

Keep a running list of supplies so you have everything you need for your next painting session.

Buy a Larger Volume of Frequently Used Supplies

If you paint often, see what supplies you use the most and buy them in larger quantities to save on costs.

Learn from Unsuccessful Paintings

As a new pour painter, try not to be discouraged by pieces that don't turn out as well as you hoped. They're just part of the learning process with this unpredictable type of art. Unsuccessful paintings can teach you what doesn't work, so you can make changes or improvements to move toward creating artwork you love.

Keep a Pour Painting Notebook or Journal

Consider using a notebook or e-document to record a few notes about each painting you complete. This can be helpful to see what materials and processes create your best work. Write the notes soon after finishing while the details are still fresh in your mind. Chapter 26 has tips on how to do this.

Keep Experimenting

With each work you finish, you'll likely think of more pouring ideas to try. There are no absolute rules for this creative painting technique, so set your imagination free.

Add New Supplies to Your Collection

There are many pour painting supplies to create mesmerizing patterns in your pours. One example is a "split cup," which has two or more channels for paint. These cups help with color separation and generate ribbon-like patterns and designs.

Other items include pour painting colanders, strainers, and flower pour cups. These supplies are available from online retailers and online arts & crafts marketplaces.

Continue Learning

Pour painting is continually evolving. Each day, painters around the world invent new ways to pour paint. The more you learn now, the better prepared you'll be to try the methods that interest you. A few options for further education include online or in-person classes, books, and videos. Also, consider learning traditional acrylic painting to complement your acrylic pouring skills.

CHAPTER 24

solving pour painting problems

EVEN WITH OUR BEST EFFORTS, THE RESULTS OF ACRYLIC POURS CAN BE unpredictable. Here are ways to identify, solve, and prevent various pour painting problems.

1. NOT ENOUGH PAINT TO COVER THE SURFACE

If there's not enough paint to cover the surface, it doesn't mean the painting is ruined. There's usually a brief window of time to fix the problem before the paint starts to dry.

Solution: If your supplies are nearby, mix more paint and medium (even just one or two colors) and pour it onto the uncovered area or areas of the painting. Next, carefully tilt the surface or use a palette knife (or craft stick) to blend the new and existing paint. Try to do this within five to seven minutes of the initial pour for the best chances of this fix being successful.

In the future, keep some pre-mixed paint in sealed bottles or containers nearby in case it's needed.

2. AIR BUBBLE TROUBLE

Air bubbles can form during paint mixing or pouring, leaving tiny pin-hole marks or indentations on the painting. Here are my tips for preventing or removing air bubbles.

Solutions:

How to Prevent Air Bubbles

- When mixing paint and pouring medium, stir slowly and gently.
- Prepare paints and pouring medium mixtures in advance and store them overnight in airtight bottles, containers, or cups covered with plastic food wrap sealed with rubber bands to let bubbles dissipate.
- Limit the use of palette knives and painting tools, as these often create air bubbles in the paint.

How to Get Rid of Air Bubbles in Poured Paint

- If a few air bubbles appear in freshly poured paint, use a round toothpick or sewing pin to pop them. This should be done carefully to avoid disturbing the rest of the painting.

Tip: It's also fine to leave air bubbles alone. Sometimes they pop on their own. Other times, they become part of the painting. They're part of what makes fluid art unique.

3. THICKER PAINT ON ONE SIDE OF THE PAINTING

If the paint has pooled on one side of the painting, the painting was done on a surface that wasn't completely level.

Solution: Use a level (or level app on a smartphone) to ensure the canvas/painting surface is even before each painting session.

4. THE PAINTING'S FINISH ISN'T SMOOTH

Here are a few causes and solutions for paintings with lumps, indentations, or other problems with their finish.

1: Dried paint or pouring medium can accumulate on bottle nozzles or caps and fall into paint mixing cups. These pieces can leave bumps or imperfections on the painting surface.

Solution: To prevent this issue in the future, wipe all paint and medium nozzles and caps before putting supplies away. Also, after the paint and pouring medium is blended, pour each mixture through a stainless-steel mesh sink strainer to filter out lumps or pieces of dried paint.

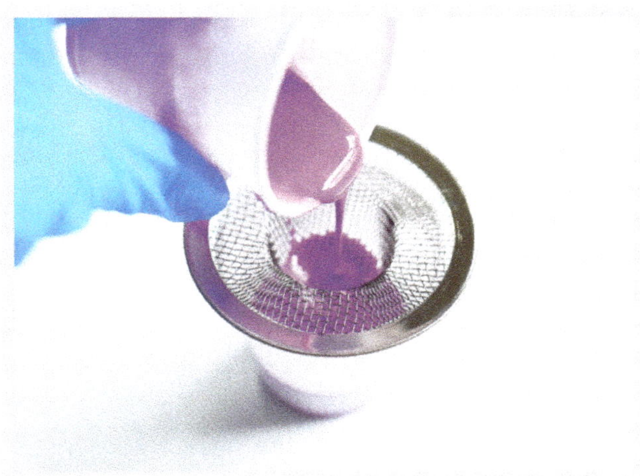

If the paint has already been poured, use a toothpick to remove the paint pieces after the painting is on a raised surface.

2: Older or dry paints or pouring medium are another possible cause of a bumpy finish.

Solution: If you suspect your products are getting dry, pour a small amount from each bottle onto a paper towel to see if any are dry, thick, or lumpy.

3: Paint mixture is too thick - If the paint's consistency is too thick for pouring, this can cause a painting with a lumpy or uneven finish.

Solution: Ensure that each color is blended to an optimal consistency. See Chapter 15 (Sections 3 and 4).

4: Moving a painting before the paint film hardens might cause ridges, ripples, or an uneven finish.

Solution: Be careful not to move or disturb the painting until it's dry.

5. CRACKS ON THE PAINTING

It's disappointing to find unsightly cracks in your painting. Here are some causes and solutions for this issue.

1: The paint dried too quickly - If the top layer of paint dries faster than the lower layers, this sometimes results in cracks and crazes on the surface.

Solution: Avoid painting in a hot workspace or in direct sunlight.

2: The paint mixtures were too thick - If the paint seemed unusually thick, this might have caused the cracks. If only one color cracked, perhaps that color was too thick.

Solution: Next time, try to ensure that all the paint mixtures are the right consistency.

3: Not enough paint was poured off the surface - Leaving too thick of a layer of paint on the painting surface can make it more susceptible to cracks.

Solution: Practice finding a balance between keeping the best parts of the painting's design on the surface and letting enough paint spill over the edges to prevent an overly thick paint film.

4: Too much water was added to the paint - Water weakens acrylic paint and may increase the chances of cracks.

Solution: If adding water to a paint mixture, try to limit the amount to less than 20 to 30% of the total volume. If possible, thin acrylic paints

using a high-quality pouring medium or a product such as Golden®
GAC 800 to reduce the likelihood of cracks.

5: Too much of an additive was used - Unless a minimal amount of an
additive is used, it sometimes causes the paint to crack.

Solution: Only put a limited amount of an additive in the paint
mixtures, as explained in Chapter 15 (Section 9).

6: Varnishing the painting before it's fully dry - If an acrylic pour
painting is varnished before the paint has enough time to cure (fully
harden), it has the potential to crack.

Solution: To be safe, wait at least three to four weeks after a painting is
finished before varnishing it.

7: Poor quality paints or pouring medium - Not all products for
pouring are the same. Using good quality products can increase the
chances that paintings will dry crack-free.

Solution: If you're unsure what to choose, read product reviews online
or ask for recommendations from other pour painters or art supply
store staff.

6. MUDDY COLORS

A painting's colors can appear muddy for multiple reasons. Here are
some causes to consider.

1: The paint mixtures are too thin - If the paint mixtures are too thin,
colors may blend too much and look muddy. This can also happen if
too much water is added to the mixture.

Solution: Try to ensure that the paints are mixed to a good consistency.
See Chapter 15 (Section 3).

2: Not enough pouring medium used - Sometimes, using an insuffi-
cient amount of pouring medium compared to paint results in muddy
colors.

Solution: Start with the paint-to-pouring medium ratio suggested on the medium bottle. If there's not one listed or if you're using an alternative medium like PVA glue or Floetrol®, try increasing the amount of medium and see if the problem improves.

3: Dark colors - Dark and intense paint colors can overtake lighter and less bold colors, resulting in darker and less colorful artwork than expected.

Solution: Limit the amount of dark and intense colors until you're familiar with how they interact with the lighter shades. It can take practice to find the right balance of colors and achieve the results you're hoping for.

4: Color Combination - Certain color combinations are more likely than others to look muddy. For example, complementary colors (colors opposite each other on the color wheel) can become muddy if they blend. Two examples are red and green, and yellow and violet.

Solutions: If you think a particular combination causes muddiness, try to avoid it in the future. Those new to mixing colors may find it easier to start with monochromatic or analogous hues. Chapter 4 provides examples.

If using complementary colors in a painting, try adding just one or two shades to see how they work together. Alternatively, use white paint as a divider between complementary colors, or pour complementary colors on opposite sides of the work so there's less chance of them blending.

It's also helpful to create small testing paintings of new color combinations before working on larger surfaces.

5: Overworked Painting - Using a palette knife or other tools to blend or move the paint sometimes causes muddy colors.

Solution: Limit the use of these tools to avoid over-blending colors.

7. I WANT TO PAINT OVER A FAILED PAINTING

There's no need to throw out a painting that doesn't meet your expectations. If the work was done on a stretched canvas, wood panel, or another surface that's durable enough to reuse, here's how to get it ready to pour a new painting over it.

Allow the old painting at least three to four weeks to fully dry. A day or two before pouring, ensure the painting surface is clean and dust-free, then apply gesso as described in Chapter 13. This will cover the old painting while priming the surface for a new layer of paint.

If silicone or other oil-based additives were used in the old painting, the oily residue must be completely removed before applying gesso. See "Removing Silicone and Oils from Paintings" in Chapter 21 (pp. 142-143) for information about how to do this.

Most of the time, removing residual oils and adding a fresh coat of gesso is enough to prepare the painting surface for a new pour. If the finish of the old painting isn't completely smooth, use a very fine grit sandpaper (#150 or #220) to smooth out any bumps or imperfections before applying gesso. For safety, it's a good idea to wear safety goggles and a sanding or respirator mask. After sanding the surface, brush off any dust before applying gesso.

8. A PAINTING WITH A DULL OR UNEVEN FINISH

Mixing and matching paints with multiple finishes (such as matte and glossy) can sometimes result in a painting with an uneven sheen. Additionally, some pouring mediums dry to a lackluster finish that doesn't accent the vibrant paint colors used.

Solution: Both problems can be solved by adding a coat of varnish to unify the finish, add an even level of shine, and brighten dull colors.

9. I CAN'T GET CELLS IN MY POURS

Many variables affect whether cells develop in the paint. There are several ways to make these colorful, bubble-like shapes more likely to appear. Here are a few I've found to work best.

1: Strive to get paint mixtures to an optimal consistency as listed in Chapter 15 (Section 3). Paint that's too thick or too thin will reduce the chances of cells forming. If cells form in paint that's too thin, they can lose their shape before the paint dries.

2: When pouring directly onto a canvas, pour the lowest density paint colors as the first layer, then add the higher density colors over them. The lighter colors will rise toward the surface, which may cause cells to form.

If creating a dirty pour cup, pour the highest density color (like titanium white) into the cup first. When pouring from this cup or using a flip cup technique, the first color will become a top layer and provide a better chance of cells.

Tip: Look online for a paint or pigment density chart for your brand of paints. Knowing the density of each color is helpful for paint layering.

3: Use a paint additive such as silicone, dimethicone, or isopropyl alcohol in the paint mixtures. See Chapter 6 and Chapter 15 (Section 9) for further information about additives.

4: Try a "swiping technique." After all the paint colors have been poured onto the painting surface, use a palette knife, a piece of cardboard, or a similar flat object to lightly skim across the surface of the wet paint. This can help release cells, especially if using an additive. Swiping a dense color like white over less dense colors can increase the chances of cells occurring.

5: Use Floetrol® as a pouring medium on its own or with silicone oil or dimethicone to increase the chances of cells.

6: Try the dirty flip cup pour in Chapter 16. It can increase the likelihood of cells.

7: Experiment with various paint, pouring medium, and additive combinations to see what works best for creating cells.

8: Observe any differences in the amount and size of cells when using minimal stirring of an additive into a mixture and more stirring.

9: Pour a sufficient amount of paint onto the surface. While tilting the canvas stretches the paint and sometimes generates cells, the cells can lose their shape or disappear if extensive tilting is needed to cover the surface.

Many beginners find it challenging to get beautiful cells in their paintings. Continued practice and experimentation are the best way to achieve your desired results.

10. I WANT TO AVOID CELLS IN MY PAINTINGS

Many artists prefer pour paintings without cells. Here are my tips for a cell-free pour:

1: Skip the paint additives, as these products encourage cell formation.

2: Stir paint and pouring medium mixtures slowly to avoid creating air bubbles. Air bubbles in the paint sometimes increase the chances of cells.

3: Wait until paint mixtures are bubble-free before pouring. This can take anywhere from twenty minutes to twelve hours or more, depending on the paint and pouring medium combination and how much stirring was done.

4: Pour enough paint onto the painting surface, so it doesn't need to be extensively tilted to distribute the paint. Tilting stretches the paint and sometimes produces cells.

5: Avoid swiping techniques or blending wet paint with a palette knife because this can create air bubbles and cells.

6: Try to pour lower density colors on top of heavier, more opaque shades. Doing the opposite can increase the chances of getting cells.

tips for photographing paintings

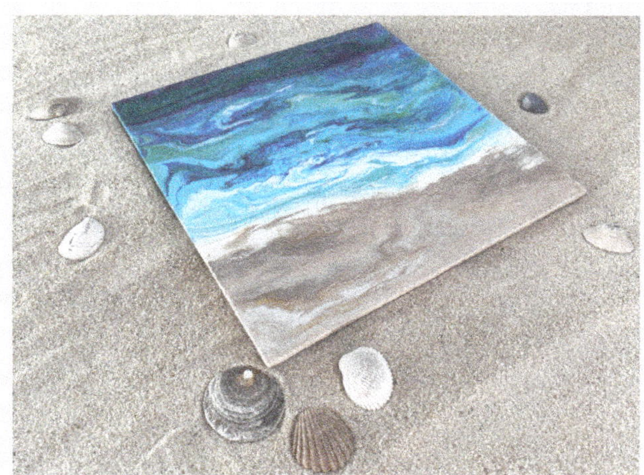

Taking photos of finished paintings is a great way to observe the progression of your skills. It also allows you to share your work online or have your favorite artwork printed on a tote bag, beverage cup, phone case, and an assortment of other custom-made merchandise at a print-on-demand website.

Here are my tips for taking and editing photos of paintings.

Taking Photos

- It's best to photograph artwork before applying varnish to avoid the glare of a glossy finish.
- Use a digital camera or smartphone that takes clear, high-resolution photos.
- To avoid using a flash, take photos in an area with lots of natural light. The ideal time of day varies by location. Photos that accurately capture the color and light of a painting will need fewer adjustments.
- Place the painting far enough from windows or light sources to prevent a surface glare. If needed, try taking a photo from a different angle or position. In rooms with natural light, there may be fewer issues with reflections or glares at certain times of the day.
- Unless a work is already framed and on a wall, it's easiest to place the painting on the floor and photograph it from above.
- If you intend to crop the image to only the painting, the background doesn't matter. Otherwise, choose something that keeps the focus on your art, such as a sheet of white or black poster board, a wood floor, or something more decorative and creative.

Editing Photos

- Use photo editing software or an app on a smartphone, tablet, or computer.
- Always edit a copy or duplicate of the photo, not the original.
- Keep the painting nearby so it can be referenced while editing the photo. This will help you make the photo look as similar as possible to the original work.
- Use the "crop" tool to crop and straighten the image as needed.
- Locate the "undo" function so any changes you don't like can be reversed.

- The "auto-correct" feature on photo editing applications automatically adjusts the color, lighting, and other key settings. If it doesn't improve the photo, undo auto-correct and adjust the settings manually.

Here are the most common settings that might need changes.

- Adjust "brightness" to increase or reduce a photo's overall light level.
- Adjust "contrast" to increase or decrease the difference between the photo's darks and lights.
- Adjust "saturation" to increase or decrease a photo's color intensity.
- Adjust "temperature" to make a photo's color tone warmer or cooler. For example, increase the temperature to correct a photo with bluish tones and reduce it to improve an image that appears too yellow.

After you're happy with the edited photo, be sure to save it.

how to start a pour painting journal

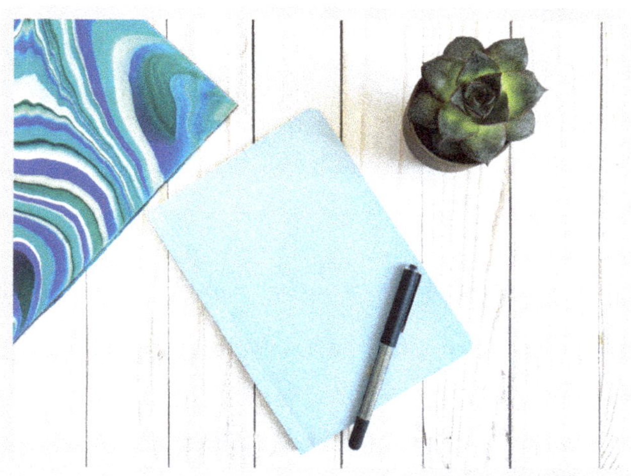

When I first started pour painting, I went through a lot of trial and error. I experimented with many paints, mediums, and techniques before I started creating artwork I was happy with. Early on, I began keeping notes for each piece I finished and found them helpful to see which products and methods worked best for me. When you discover a winning combination of supplies, colors, or techniques, having notes lets you replicate what worked well to enjoy success with other paintings.

This type of journal is also beneficial for seeing where improvement is needed. Identifying the areas that need work will allow you to correct problems and move beyond the beginner phase more quickly.

Pour painting journals aren't for everyone, so if your style is more spontaneous, or if this doesn't sound like something you want to try, skip this section and keep doing what works for you.

The example below offers ideas and suggestions about what to record. This is only a general guide, so customize it to whatever you find pertinent. Notes can be as brief or detailed as you like and written in a notebook or an e-document.

Pour Painting Journal

Date: List the date the painting was done.

Description: Write a line to identify the painting, including the surface type and size. Example: *Purple, Aqua, and Silver Puddle Pour with Cells on a 12-inch Square Canvas*

Surface Prep Notes: Mention if gesso or other products were used to prepare the painting surface.

Paint Type and Brand: List the paint type and brand or brands used.

Paint Colors: List the specific paint colors used. Optionally, record the amount of paint in each paint cup.

Pouring Medium: List the brand or brands of pouring medium used. If you like, list the amount.

Paint-to-Pouring Medium Ratio or Recipe/Formula: If you used a specific paint-to-pouring medium ratio, recipe, or formula, list that here.

Water Added: Record the amount of water put into the mixture, if applicable.

Paint Additive: Note any additive and amount used, if applicable.

Consistency: Describe the consistency of the paint mixture.

Pouring Technique or Method: List the technique or pouring method used, such as "Traditional Pour" or "poured colors from plastic bottles."

Tools: Note any tools used in the painting's creation, such as a palette knife or craft stick.

Process Notes: Record the details about how you did the painting that you wish to remember. For example, "Poured colors in large spirals across the canvas."

Varnish/Finish: If the painting was varnished, note the product or products used and the date it was applied.

Result: Record a quick summary of how the painting turned out. Mention anything you especially like or dislike about it.

"Next time, I Would…": List anything you would have done differently. This can be related to color choices, materials, the paint-to-pouring medium ratio, or any other aspect of the painting or process. If this doesn't apply, skip it.

New Ideas: Completing one painting may lead to ideas for others. Capture these thoughts to remember them for your future creations.

Supplies to Buy: Note supplies you've used up or are getting low on. Add them to your shopping list so they're available for your next painting session.

Other: Use this section to note anything that doesn't fit elsewhere. Some ideas include color combinations you'd like to try or new pouring techniques you want to learn.

Photo: Add a photo to identify the work and see how your skills improve with each painting you complete.

closing

I hope this book has been a helpful starting point on your acrylic pour painting journey, and these lessons and tips will inspire you to continue exploring this intriguing and limitless style of art.

glossary of acrylic pour painting terms

Acrylic Ink - Inks made with ultra-fine color pigments that are water-resistant or waterproof, depending on the brand

Acrylic Paint - A water-based paint that dries quickly and can be used for many types of painting and artwork

Acrylic Polymer Varnish - A non-removable, water-based varnish that helps protect paintings from UV light, dust, fading, and discoloration

Acrylic Resin Varnish - A removable, solvent-based varnish that dries to a hard, clear finish and helps protect paintings from UV light, dust, fading, and discoloration

Additive - A liquid product such as silicone oil, dimethicone, or isopropyl alcohol added to acrylic paint mixtures to encourage cells to form in wet paint

Archival Quality - Something expected to last a long time with proper care and conditions

Artist Grade - A professional quality product, also called artist quality

Base Coat - A layer of paint and pouring medium mixture poured over the entire painting surface before pouring the primary colors of the painting

Bookbinding Glue - A type of adhesive used for bookbinding that can serve as an alternative pouring medium for acrylic pours

Cells - Assorted round shapes that sometimes develop in wet acrylic paint

Composition - The arrangement of the various elements in a piece of artwork

Crazing - Small crevices that can form on a painting's surface if the paint dries unevenly

Dimethicone - A type of silicone used in some hair serums and skin care products that can be added to pour painting mixtures to aid in cell formation

Dirty Pour - A pour painting technique where multiple paint colors are poured into a single cup and then poured onto a painting surface

Floetrol® - A latex-based house paint additive that works as an alternative pouring medium for acrylic pour painting

Gesso - A primer used to prepare a painting surface and improve paint adherence

Gloss Medium - A multi-purpose fluid acrylic medium used in pour painting as a pouring medium or to seal wood panels, rocks, and other porous painting surfaces

Heavy Body Acrylic Paint - A thick, high-viscosity type of acrylic paint commonly used for traditional acrylic painting

Hue - A pure color on the color wheel

Iridescent - A light-reflecting, pearl-like shimmer and sparkle

Isolation Coat - A clear coating applied to a finished painting before the final varnish, which protects the paint if the varnish ever needs to be removed

Isopropyl Alcohol - A common antiseptic that can be used as an additive in acrylic paint mixtures to help produce cells and cellular patterns in pour paintings

Lightfast - The ability of a product to last without fading from light exposure over time

Liquid Acrylic Paint - A low viscosity acrylic paint in a fluid, pourable form

Matte - A flat, shine-free finish

Multi-purpose PVA Glue - A polyvinyl acetate glue that works as an alternative pouring medium for acrylic pours

Negative Space - The vacant space around or between the primary subject or design of a painting

Paint Density - The weight of the color pigment and other ingredients of a specific paint color

Painting Surface - The material used to paint on, such as a stretched canvas, wood panel, or ceramic tile

Palette Knife - A painting tool, typically metal or plastic, that can be used for blending or moving paint around on the painting surface

Permanent Varnish - A non-removable varnish that becomes a permanent part of the artwork

Pouring Medium - A fluid product that's mixed with acrylic paints before pouring to enhance the paint and extend its volume without diluting the color

Pre-Mixed Acrylic Paints - Pour-ready acrylic paints with pouring medium pre-added

Removable Varnish - A varnish that can be removed with paint thinner or other products suitable for varnish removal

Self-Leveling - A product that spreads out evenly to provide a smooth, level finish

Silicone Oil - A type of oil added to acrylic pouring mixtures to help cells form in the paint

Traditional Pour - A pour painting technique in which paint colors are poured directly from individual cups onto the painting surface

Value - The relative lightness or darkness of a color

Varnish - A clear finish that helps protect completed artwork from physical and environmental damage

Viscosity - The relative thickness of paint, consistency

<h1 style="text-align:center; font-family:cursive;">about the author</h1>

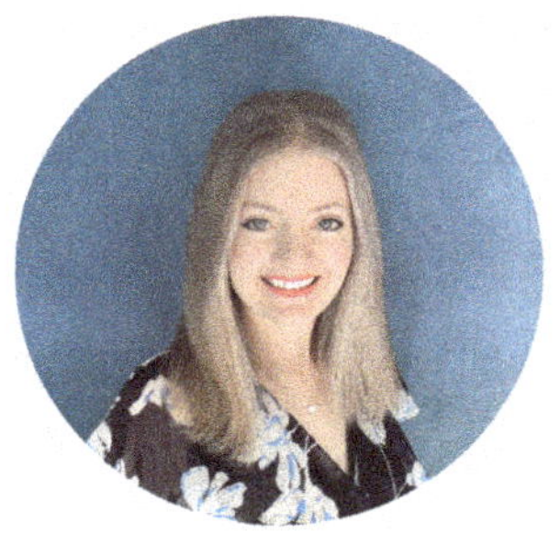

Carrie Kelley is an author and artist from the United States. Her interest in all things creative goes back as far as she can remember. From her earliest years, she loved every type of art she tried and took classes in everything from sketching and painting to comic book drawing and pottery. By the time she was ten years old, she'd won numerous local and national art competitions. While pursuing her B.A. in Communications, she took art classes at the University of Miami in Florida and Cleveland Institute of Art. After graduation, she completed a graphic design certification program.

Several years ago, she discovered acrylic pour painting and became fascinated with this unique and expressive style of art. Using her decades of traditional acrylic painting experience and lots of trial and error, she taught herself the ins and outs of creating colorful paintings using fluid art techniques. In 2018, she began writing online articles and tutorials about pour painting to share her knowledge and passion for this topic with others. *Acrylic Pour Painting: A Beginner's Guide with Instructions, Ideas, and Tips for Creating Unique Abstract Paintings* is her first book.

also by carrie kelley

Acrylic Pouring Logbook & Journal: A Notebook for Your Painting Projects